A BOOK
OF
VULGAR
VERSE

checkerbooks

checkerbooks inc.
TORONTO CANADA
Printed in the United States of America

INTRODUCTION

THE GENTLEMAN ABOUT TOWN has performed a service of notable worth in preserving and giving definitive form to the wealth of latter-day folk-lore which is contained within the covers of this book. "American folk-lore has of necessity sought cover, driven by the undiscriminating tirades and sadistic tyrannies of the Mrs. Grundys who are an irremovable part of this melange we know as modern civilization. Undoubtedly, much material of permanent literary value has been lost.

Literary worth in folk-lore depends on just one thing—its spontaneity. Folk-lore is no hot-house plant, to be fertilized with refined chemicals and maintained at constant temperature when the winds of reality blow. On the contrary, folk-lore seeks its nourishment in the fertilizing essences of nature, and springs triumphantly forth no matter how fierce the winds or how rigorous the frost. Just as some beautiful plants seem to grow in opposition to all efforts of the gardeners and the horticulturists, so does folk-lore thrive in the face of determined efforts of the sentimentalists to deny its very existence.

Folk-lore is, after all, nothing but the literature of the people. It, more truly than any more polished side of literary effort, reflects the *average* standard of all the people at the time of its currency. The very fact of its existence is dependent upon the willingness of the people (not of the literary guildmasters) to keep it alive. Literature with a capital "L" has all the stabilizing factors of the printed word and of learned tradition to perpetuate it—folk-lore lives only in the voices of the people themselves—the source from which the material in this book has been drawn, from cover to cover.

However, good taste has nothing in common with good folk-lore. One is artificial, the other natural. One is the essence of refinement, the other is the rawest of raw material. The one is the glossy veneer, all external handsomeness, the other the sturdy fabric from which all strength is drawn. In fact, almost all good folk-lore (and by that I mean all real folk-lore) is in distinct bad taste in drawing rooms and among the niceties of society. It is as much an outcropping of underlying fundamental strength as those deep-rooted rocks which are the farmer's despair even though they be the ribs of the earth.

These "Immortalia" are homely; they are imaginative; they are couched in the most vigorous of language; they are crude in literary form, oftentimes; yet they are what people—just ordinary people, undistinguished and unknown,—have been thinking and saying and singing for their own delectation during the last seventy-five years.

This is not a book for the tender-skinned, nor for those excellent persons (and their name is legion!) who sincerely prefer to keep their thoughts within the strict bounds of conventionality. It is, instead, an effort of serious contribution to the history of peoples, and a book for the enjoyment of those who can prize the lily and forget the odorous yet fertile dung-heap from which it springs. It is a book for those who acknowledge that the dung-heap is as indispensable in the scheme of biology as is the drawing-room—and that in its way, even the dung-heap has virtues and can produce immaculate lilies.

If you are squeamish about reading the Anglo-Saxon biological unisyllables—if you prefer to believe that children come out of the blue rather than as a result of biological processes—if you feel that nothing between neck and knees should even have a name—then close this book now, and read no further.

But if, instead, you have an enlightened sense of humor—if you admit the truth about the human body in its essentials as readily as you do about it in its extremities—if names to you are titles by which factual things are known—if profanity is to you the name of a class of words, and not an implication of polluting horrors—then prize this book above rubies, for it is for you that it has been made.

The Gentleman About Town asks me to make acknowledgements on his behalf to the many ladies and gentlemen who have assisted him in this compilation; and to express his regret that circumstances deter him from giving them their proper share of thanks by naming them here.

THE GENTLEMAN FROM OUT OF TOWN.

THE SKONK I HUNT

Anonymous

I hunt de bear, I hunt de moose,
　An' sometam hunt de rat;
Las' week I take ma hax an' go
　For hunt a skonk polecat.

Ma fren' Beel say he's ver' fine fur,
　An' sametam good to heat;
I tell ma wife I get fur coat,
　Sametam I get some meat.

I walk 'bout three, five, six mile,
　An' then I feel strong smell—
Tink mebbe that dam skonk she **die**
　An' fur coat gone to hell.

Purrsoon bime-by I see that skonk
　Close up by one beeg tree;
I sneek up ver' close behin',
　I tink he no see me.

Bime-by I'm ver', ver' close,
　I raise ma hax up high,
Dat goddam skonk he up an' plunk—
　T'row something in my eye.

Oh, Sacre Bleu! I tink I blin';
　Jees Chris! I cannot see;
I run roun' an' roun' an' roun'
　'Till I bump in goddam tree.

Bime-by I drop ma hax away
　An' light out for de shack,
I tink 'bout million skonk
　He clim' up on ma back.

1

Ma wife she meet at de door,
　　She sic on me de dog;
She say, "You no sleep here tonight,
　　Go out an' sleep with hog."

I try to get in that pig-pen,
　　Jees Christ! now what you tink?
Dat goddam hog no stan' for that
　　On 'count of awful stink.

No more I go for hunt de skonk
　　To get his fur an' meat;
For if he peese he smell so bad;
　　Jees Chris! what if he sheet!

～

NOW MY FAIR BRIDE

Anonymous

Now my fair bride, now will I storm the mint
Of love and joy, and rifle all that's in it.
Now my enfranchised hand on every side
Shall o'er thy naked polished ivory slide;
Freely shall my longing eyes behold
Thy bared snow and thy undrained gold;
No curtain now, tho' of transparent lawn,
Shall be before thy virgin treasure drawn;
I will enjoy thee now, my fairest; come
And fly with me to Love's elysium.
My rudder with thy bold hand, like a try'd
And skilful pilot, thou shalt steer, and guide
My bark in Love's dark channel, where it shall
Dance as the rising waves do rise and fall.
Whilst mine tall pinnace in the Cyprian strait
Rides safe at anchor and unlades the freight.

2

THE BALLAD OF GAFFER HEPELTHWAITE

Anonymous

Far inland from the lighthouse where the angry tempests rage
Resides old Gaffer Hepelthwaite who drives the Essex stage,—
A man of many winters and so vigorous withal
That coy spermatozoa still inhabit his left ball.

Alas for Gaffer Hepelthwaite! so virile was his stroke,
So stern and stiff his penis like the mighty Essex oak,
That never yet a maiden did confront his aged e'en
Whose legs he did not yearn to part and place his prong between.

One day the Mayor of Essex town upon his good roan mare
Came riding down the turnpike to enjoy the Autumn air,
And with his great official rode his winsome daughter Bess
Whose passion for Fall atmosphere was but a trifle less.

"Trot-trot! Along they cantered—quoth the Mayor, "Ecod, my lass,
"They tell me Gaffer Hevelthwaite can still enjoy his ass."
"O pish!" exclaimed the damosel, and lustily laughed she,
"No fond octogenarian could ever diddle me!"

A rattle interrupted her—a clatter as of feet—
The Essex stage swept into view, the Gaffer in his seat.
"What ho!" the Mayor shouted, "Pause in your headlong flight,
For here's a pretty argument which you can set aright."
They made him explanation and witthout the least ado,

This aged, snowy-headed wight his prick brought into view.
The damosel dismounted and the Gaffer climbed on top,
And proved the Mayor's contention till that worthy ordered, "Stop!"

"Stop, did you say, your worship?" said the Gaffer 'tween his strokes,
Administering to Bessie five final lusty pokes,
"I pray you, noble gentleman, this order to rescind,
For I find I'm just arriving at my famous second wind."

3

'Twas then that Gaffer Hepelthwaite, his penis in the air,
Committed violent outrage on the gentle young roan mare,
And finding that she wearied, next proceeded to engage
The splendid span of animals connected with the stage.

.　.　.　.　.　.

'Twas twilight over Essex town; the damsel and her sire
In the Mayor's habitation were preparing to retire.
"What cheer, my lass?" the father quoth, and, "Cheer enough"
　　quoth she,
"For I shall ride the Essex stage as long as stage there be."

OH, I MET MISS MALONE
Anonymous

Oh, I met Miss Malone in the graveyard,
　And I laid Miss Malone on a stone;
And when I socked each stroke to her,
　You could hear all the dead people moan.

Oh, I met Miss Malone in the barnyard,
　And she was all covered with mud;
And when I asked what had happened,
　She said she'd been climbed by a stud.

THE PASSING OF THE BACKHOUSE

JAMES WHITCOMB RILEY

When memory keeps me company and moves to smiles or tears,
A weather-beaten object looms through the mist of years.
Behind the house and barn it stood, a half a mile or more,
And hurrying feet a path had made up to its swinging door.
Its architecture was a type of simple classic art,
But in the tragedy of life it played a leading part.
And oft the passing traveller drove slow and heaved a sigh,
To see the modest hired girl slip out with glances shy.

We had our posey garden that the women loved so well,
I loved it too, but better still I loved the stronger smell
That filled the evening breezes so full of homely cheer,
And told the night-o'ertaken tramp that human life was near.
On August afternoons, it made a little bower
Delightful, where my grandsire sat and whiled away an hour.
For there the Summer morning its very cares entwined,
And berry bushes reddened in the streaming soil behind.

All day fat spiders spun their webs to catch the buzzing flies
That flitted to and from the house, where ma was baking pies.
And once a swarm of hornets bold had built a palace there,
And stung my unsuspecting aunt—I must not tell you where.
Then father took a flaming pole—that was a happy day—
He nearly brrned the building up—the hornets left to stay.
When Summer's bloom began to fade and Winter to carouse,
We banked the little building with a heap of hemlock boughs.

But when the crust was on the snow and sullen skies were gray
In sooth the building was no place where one could wish to stay,
We did our duties promptly, there one purpose swayed the mind;
We tarried not, nor lingered long on what we left behind.
The torture of that icy seat would make a Spartan sob,
For needs must scrape the gooseflesh with a lacerating cob.
That from a frost-encrusted nail did dangle by a string—
My father was a frugal man and wasted not a thing.

When grandpa had "to go out back" and make his morning call,
We'd bundle up the dear old man with a muffler and a shawl.
I knew the hole on which he sat—'twas padded all around,
And once I dared to sit there—'twas all too wide I found.
My loins were all too little, and I jack-knifed there to stay.
They had to come and get me out, or I'd have passed away.
Then father said ambition was a thing that boys should shun,
And I just used the children's hole 'til childhood days were done.

And still I marvel at the craft that cut those holes so true,
The baby hole, and the slender hole that fitted sister Sue.
That dear old country landmark;—I've tramped around a bit,
And in the lap of luxury my lot has been to sit,
But ere I die I'll eat the fruit of trees I robbed of yore,
Then seek the shanty where my name is carved upon the door.
I ween the old familiar smell will soothe my jaded soul,
I'm now a man, but, none the less, I'll try the children's hole.

IN YOUR BOYHOOD DAYS

Anonymous

First you knock at the door, and then you ask for Annie
Then you put a nickel in the old piannie;
And down comes Annie in her dirty silk kimonie,
All dolled up with perfume and colognie;
Then you pay a dollar for a bottle of beerie,
Another dollar goes for the music you hearie,
Three dollars more, and up you go with dearie;
And then you've got nine days of doubt and fearie!

6

A SEVENTY YEAR OLD FOLLOWER

Anonymous

An old sport lounged in a grandstand chair,
There was dung in his whiskers and hay in his hair,
And his voice rang hoarse on the sultry air,
   "He'll win in a walk, b'Jesus!"
"Just wait 'til you see them turn him loose,
He'll go through that field like shit through a goose,
He'll do it as easy as *ace* takes a *deuce*—
   He'll win in a walk, b'Jesus!"

"His breeding is right, he can't go slow,
He's out of Black Bess by Hungry Joe;
Of that bunch of skates he'll sure make a show—
   He'll win in a walk, b'Jesus!"

"I ain't got no money, but if I was rich,
I'd go dead broke on that son-of-a-bitch;
When he gets a-goin' he'll make 'em all itch—
   He'll win in a walk, b'Jesus!"

"They've sent 'em away—gave him worst of the start—
It don't make no difference—he don't care a fart—
The suckers are yellow but he's game—got a heart—
   He'll win in a walk, b'Jesus!"

"From the nineteenth position way out in the grass
Where weeds are so tall they tickle his ass,
He's just nosed out of place Scotch Highland Lass—
   He'll win in a walk, b'Jesus!"

"They are swung in the stretch and the bastard is third—
He has worked up to second—now, he's slipped on a terd;
He's slipped in the ditch, the son-of-a-bitch—
   He wasn't in it, b'Jesus!"

LADY LIL

EUGENE FIELD

Lil was the best our camp perduced;
And of all the gents what Lillian goosed,
None had no such goosin', nor never will,
Since the Lord raked in poor Lady Lil.
We had a bet in our town
Thar warn't no geezer that could brown
Lil toa finish, any style—
And no bloke ever made the trial
'Cept Short Pete, the halfbreed galoot,
Who wandered in from Scruggins' Chute.
His takin' it surprised us all,
For Pete he warn't so big nor tall,
But when he yanked his tool out thar,
And laid it out across the bar,
We 'lowed our Lil had met her fate,
But thar warn't no backin' out that late,
And so we 'ranged to have the mill
Behind the whore-house on the hill,
Where all the boys could get a seat
And watch that half-breed brown his meat.
Lil's start was like the gentle breeze
That swayed the noddin' cypress trees,
But when het up, she screwed for keeps
And laid her victims out in heaps.
She tried her twists and double biffs,
And all such m'neuvres known to quiffs,
But Pete war thar with every tack,
And kept a-lettin' out more jack.
It made us cocksmen fairly sick
To see that half-breed shove his prick.
She gave short Pete a lively mill,
And wore the grass half off the hill;
'Til finally, she missed her shot,
And Short Pete had her on the pot,
But she died game, just let me tell,
And had her boots on when she fell,
So what the hell, Bill, what the hell!

8

LITTLE WILLIE*

EUGENE FIELD

When Willie was a little boy,
  Not more than five or six,
Right constantly did he annoy
  His mother with his tricks,
Yet not a picayune cared I
  For what he did or said,
Unless, as happened frequently,
  The rascal wet the bed.

Closely he cuddled up to me,
  And put his hands in mine,
'Til all at once I seemed to be
  Afloat in seas of brine.
Sabean odors clogged the air,
  And filled my soul with dread,
Yet I could only grin and bear
  When Willie wet the bed.

'Tis many times that rascal has
  Soaked all the bedclothes through,
Whereat I'd feebly light the gas
  And wonder what to do.
Yet there he'd lie, so peaceful like;
  God bless his curly head;
I quite forgave the little tyke
  For wetting of the bed.

Ah me, those happy days have flown;
  My boy's a father too,
And little Willies of his own
  Do what he used to do.
And I! Ah, all that's left of me
  Is dreams of pleasure fled;
Our boys ain't what they used to be
  When Willie wet the bed.

Had I my choice, no shapely dame
    Should share my couch with me,
No amorous jade of tarnished fame,
    No wench of high degree;
But I should choose and choose again
    The little curly head
Who cuddled close beside me when
    He used to wet the bed.

*Field said his wife took the boy away on a visit,
and he found, in his absence, he couldn't sleep 'til
he got up and poured hot water on his shirt.

KING DAVID

EUGENE FIELD

David with a single stone the great Goliath slew,
But when he fucked Uriah's wife he found he needed two.

LOT

EUGENE FIELD

When good old Lot
A babe begot
Upon each lovely daughter,
He didn't wake
His ass to shake,
But slept on as he oughter.

10

SOCRATIC LOVE*

EUGENE FIELD

The story goes that Socrates, that wise Atthenian codger,
Carried, concealed about his clothes, a rare avis dodger,
Wherewith he used, when as he felt particularly nippy,
To ransack holes that did not appertain to his Xantippe.
Young Alcibiades, they say, was such a pink of fashion,
As to excite old Socrates into a flame of passion,
Which spurred him not Xantippewards to coddle and to hug 'er,
But filled him with a violent and lewd desire to bugger.

Now wit ye well that in those parts 'twas not considered nasty
For sage philosophers to turn their tools to pederasty.
The sapient Plato, whom they called in those old times The Master,
Did know a tergo, as they say, a pretty boy, hight Aster;
And old Diogenes, who thrived by raising of the dickens,
Was wont to occupy all bums, from pupils down to chickens;
Whilst that revered and austere man, the great and pious Solon,
Did penetrate a Thracian youth unto his transverse colon.
In short, it was the usual thing for horny Greeks to diddle
This gummy vent, instead of that with which the ladies piddle.

Now Alcibiades was tall and straight as any arrow;
His buttocks thrilled old Socrates unto his very marrow.
No hairs as yet profaned the vale that cleft those globes asunder,
No hairs to stay the fetid breath of bogborymal thunder,
No hairs to interrupt the course of his diurnal ordure
And gather from that excrement a rank dilberric bordure.
His sphincter was as fair a band, so Socrates protested,
As ever kept one's victuals in, or passed them undigested.

No hemorrhoids had ever marred its soft and sensuous beauty,
And on its virgin fords no prick had spent its pleasing duty;
Like some sweet bud it nested there; the winds blew gently through it
Scenting the breeze; Old Socrates more madly longed to do it.

But Alcibiades was wont to make absurd objection
When Socrates proposed the scheme of forming a connection.
The youth conceived the childish whim that buggery was nasty,
And kept the horny old philosopher from being hasty.
And so he grew from day to day, his bum waxed hourly fatter,
And Socrates was nearly dead to get at that fecal matter.

It so befell thtat on a day in sweaty summer weather,
They walked into the Acropolis quite casually together;
And as they walked the youth bent down to tie his sandal laces—
They always come unloosed, you know, at meanest times and places—
And as he stooped he lifted high and left without protection
The virgin tract of his lower gut from pod to sigmoid flexion.
For weeks and months old Socrates had had a priapism,
His pond'rous ods, a sight for Gods, were both surcharged with gism
Seeing that bum and his first chance, he made up his mind to spot 'em
So he hit 'em a lick with his Attic prick, and occupied Alcy's bottom

In vain the poor Athenian boy begged, bellowed, pissed and farted
Full twenty minutes 'lapsed before his friend and he were parted.
And while old Socrates explored the tantalizing glories
Of rugae and plicae, and quivering levatores,
The victim of his lust cried out: "Ehue, that all in vain I
Should to this hour have kept intact my rosy sphincter ani.
Fool that I was to keep it sweet and clean for this old odger!
With his three-cornered velper and his greasy balls to rodger!
Why did I not yield up my charms to Xenophon's embraces?
As I have had the chance to do at divers times and places?
Why not have given up my wealth of callipygous treasure
To handsome Cimon's burning lust or pious Plato's pleasure?
How would these men have gloried in my coy and virgin rectum,
With nary thought of vagrant dung, or cundoms to protect 'em;
But now, ye Gods, this lecherous goat with sardonic sculduggery
Doth rive my arse in twain with his incarnate god of buggery,
And when he pulls the pintle out with which just now he shuts in
The sigh my liver longs to vent, how shall I keep my guts in?"

12

Thus railed the youth against the fate that threatened to undo him;
But Soc, all heedless of his cries, right briskly socked it to him.
He packed his sperm so firmly in that colon soft and callow,
That when thereafter Alcy pooped the poop was mostly tallow.

*Written for and recited before the Papyrus Club of Boston in September, 1888.

IN IMITATION OF ROBERT HERRICK ON JULIA UNLACING HERSELF

EUGENE FIELD

Tell, if thou canst, and truly, whence doth come
   This camphire, storax, spikenard, galbanum;
These musks, these ambers, and those other smells
   Sweet as the vestrie of the oracles.
I'll tell thee: While my Julia did unlace
   Her silken bodice, but a breathing space,
The passing air such odor then assum'd,
   As when to Jove great Juno goes perfum'd,
Whose pure immortal body doth transmit
   A scent that fills both heaven and earth with it.

     'Tis when my Julia sheds her hose
     That there is wafted to my nose
    An odor with such spices fraught
     That I esteem all others naught;
    And when she belches, what a smell
     Of heliotrope and asphodel;
    But when my Julia breaks her wind,
     There issues from her fair behind
    A breath that would become, I ween,
     A Pallas or a Paphian Queen;

13

No hollow clamor speaks the birth
Of this etherial child of earth,
But hot and swift it mounts the air,
    Dispensing savour everywhere;
Swooning with ecstacy, I kiss
The heaven that breathed this gale of bliss.

PARODY ON THE OLD OAKEN BUCKET
EUGENE FIELD

How dear to my heart is the oldfashioned harlot
When fond recollection presents her to view,
The madam, the whorehouse, and beer by the carlot,
And e'en the delight of the oldfashioned screw.
You may talk as you like of these new innovations
Imported from France and of which I've heard tell,
But give me the natural, carnal sensations
Of the oldfashioned harlot wohse surname was Belle.

How dear to my heart was the oldfashioned harlot
As she lay legs outstretched on her sumptuous bed,
While I, an imptuous horny young varlet,
Drove my dink to the hub in her spoiled maidenhead;
With her musk and her smile and her very bad grammar
She had cast over me quite a Paphian spell,
And I dearly delighted to fondle and cram her,
This oldfashioned harlot whose surname was Belle.

How dear to my heart was the oldfashioned harlot
Whose regular price was five dollars a leap,—
I was really quite fond of those women in scarlet
With whom I was wont, on occasion, to sleep;
You may sing as you please of the oldfashioned bucket
That hung or that swung in the moss-girdled well,
But give me a strumpet with leisure to fuck it
Like the oldfashioned harlot whose surname was Belle.

THE FAIR LIMOUSIN

EUGENE FIELD

Since Butler sang of dildoes, and Villon loved to treat
Of certain cross-grained margots whom he'd rogered on the street;
Since Rabelais and Rochester and Chaucer chose to sing
Of that which gave them subtle joy—that is to say, *the thing,*
Why should not I, an humble bard, be pardoned if I write
Of a certain strange occurence which has lately come to light?

One evening in December, on the Boulevard de Prix,
While the sombre bells of Notre Dame announced the hour of six,
A dapper wight named Edward met, tripping on her way,
A madam with a character and a gown quite decollte;
A babbling, buxom, blooming, billowy-bubbied dame,
Camille Maria Jesus Hector Limousin, by name.

Though fair she was of countenance, she was a lewd a bitch
As ever wallowed in a bed or mouzled in a ditch;
And maugre wealth or family, she was a foul a minx
As ever fondled scabby cods or nursed gangrescent dinks.
She tumbled one American, and with his drooling yard
The august house of *Grevy* fell, and fell almighty hard.
She toyed with Simon's senile tape, and burned Clemenceau's tail;
With howling Rochefort had she drunk of Mother Watkin's ale.
With Perier, and with Carnot, she had wrestled for a fall;
She had drained old Goulet 'til he lay, no good, against the wall.
She did not swive for sustenance, she rather lived to swive,
And at the two-backed feast she beat the veriest whore alive.

No prurient dame of high degree, no wench of tarnished fame,
Could be compared with Limousin at this close-buttock game.
The Greeks had sixteen postures, and the Hindoos sixty-four,
And Cleopatra's agregate was seventy-five or more.
What were a hundred postures to this fantastic queen?
She had at least a thousand, and each of them *tres bien.*

On top, the pumping method, or lying on the side,
Or spread upon her billowy bum, a la the blushing bride,
Or standing up, or sitting down, or resting on all four,
Whereby the visitor could take his choice of either door;
Or dressed, or naked, every way her genius could invent
To catch the silvery substance that tickleth when 'tis spent.

She'd nig-nog, duffle, snuggle, concomitate and quag;
She'd dance "The Shaking of the Sheets," fadoodle, wap and shag
She'd "Come the Caster," niggle, jerk, and "Hear the Nightingale;
She'd nest-hide, dance "St. Leger's Round," and do it with her tail;
She'd break her leg above the knee, pound, click and tread as well,
And with a Holy Father, put the Devil into Hell.

She'd wrestle, bang, cohabit, futuore, cram and jig,
Jumme, copulate, accompany, swive, fornicate and frig;
Go goosing or grousing, and if needs be cooning go,
Rasp, roger, diddle, bugger, screw, canoodle, kife and mow.
There was no form of harlotry, nor any size of tarse,
That had not run the gauntlet 'twixt her nostrils and her arse.

What shall I term that slimy pit-like orifice of sin,
That let her liquefactions out, and other factions in?
A tuppence, twitchet, coney, commodity or nock,
Pudendum, titmouse, dummel-herd, quaint merkin, naf or jock?
Call it whatever please you, there's nothing in a name,
And though it had been dubbed a rose, it would have smelt the sam

And he? He was as fine a buck as ever topped a ewe,
Or with his facile penis clave a virgin's clam in two.
The flush of lusty manhood lent its beauty to his face,
And the outlines of his sturdy frame were full of virile grace.
But what seemed fairer far than these, to Limousin's fair eyes,
Was the ne plus ultra velper that swung between his thighs.

16

To this illustrious pego and its adjacent flop,
Let other kingoes, lobs, and yards, in adoration drop;
These other virgas, placket-rackets, pintles, stunts and jocks,
And all the brood of priapismic, candidates for pox;
Fie, on the mewing mentulae, for what, oh, what were these
Beside that phallic glory that hung below his knees?

Your pillycocks are competent for tickling mouses' ears,
And tools hight lobs are brute enough to bring forth bridal tears,
But the velper that's ambitious to enact heroic roles
Must be of such proportions as to stretch the roomiest holes;
With dornicks so proficient that when they cease to spout,
The lady cannot pee the dose but has to cough it out.

This tool of his was one foot long, and had three corners to it;
Its beveled velvet head stood up, when in the mood to do it,
And as it stood, and breathed and purred, and murmured sort o' sadly,
What woman, if she felt at all, but hankered for it madly?
And then, those cods, when dainty hands in amorous dalliance
          squeezed 'em,
They'd throw a stream which, ladies say, beyond all telling
          pleased 'em.

This monumental penis had frigged through all creation,
The jibby, bouser, beagle, bawd of every nation;
The courtesan, the concubine, the siren and the harlot,
The widow in her grassy weeds, the splatter-dash in scarlet;
The madam in her drawing-room, with social homage honored,
The washee-washee almond eye, whose quim is cat-a-cornered.

From Colorado in the West, to Mannheim in the East,
(And that's a goodly distance—six thousand miles at least)
This prick had mown a swath of twats of every size and age,
So numerous I could not write their number on this page.
Wher'er he went he left behind a gory, gummy trail
Of lascerated, satiated, ripped-up female tail.

17

'Twas to the bearer of this tool that Limousin applied
For the pleasant little service that he'd never yet denied,
And when she asked him, "Voulez?" he was fly enough to see
He would have to meet a crisis, so he bravely answered, "Oui!"
A crisis is a crisis, but a French one, we've heard tell,
Out-crises all crises, and that is simply Hell.

He modestly unfolded his brodbingnagian prick,
And hit that foreign madam's thing just one gosh-awful lick;
She gave a grewsome tremor, and shrieked aloud, "Mon Dieu!"
Her eyeballs rolled up in her head, her lips turned black and blue;
But there she lay and sozzled 'till he pumped her full, and then
He went and hired a doctor to sew her up again.

I'D BE SATISFIED WITH LIFE: A PAROD

Anonymous

All I want is fifty thousand women,
Giving all their earnings right to me;
And then I want a harem of good-lookers—
If all the girls on Mason Street
Would only be right true to me—
If I only had just fifty tons of yen-she;
If I never thought I had to go
To Byron Hot Springs, then I know
That I'd be satisfied with life!

LYDIA PINKHAM

Anonymous

Have you ever heard of Lydia Pinkham
  And her compound so refined,
It turns pricks to flowing fountains
And makes cunts grow on behind.

Then we'll sing, we'll sing,
We'll sing of Lydia Pinkham,
  Saviour of the human race,
How she makes, she bottles,
She sells her vegetable compound,
  And the papers publish her face.

Widow Brown, she had no children,
  Though she loved them very dear,
So she took, she swallowed, she gargled,
    Some Vegetable Compound,
  And now she has them twice a year!

Chorus—

Willie Smith had peritonitis,
  And he couldn't piss at all,
So he took, he swallowed, he gargled,
    Some Vegetable Compound,
  And now he's a human waterfall.

Chorus—

Mrs. Jones had rotten kidneys;
  Poor old lady couldn't pee,
So she took, she swallowed, she gargled,
    Some Vegetable Compound,
  And now they pipe her to the sea.

Chorus—

Geraldine, she had no breastworks,
  And she couldn't fill her blouse,
So she took, she swallowed, she gargled,
    Some Vegetable Compound,
  And now they milk her with the cows.

Chorus—

Arthur White had been castrated,
  And had not a single nut,
So he took, he swallowed, he gargled,
    Some Vegetable Compound,
  And now they hang all 'round his but.

Chorus—

Walter Black was a bearded lady,
  And his pecker wouldn't peck,
So he took, he swallowed, he gargled,
    Some Vegetable Compound,
  Now it's as long as gy-raffe's neck.

Chorus—

A TOAST

Anonymous

Here's to the men!
When I meet 'em, I like 'em,
When I like 'em, I kiss 'em,
When I kiss 'em, I love 'em,
When I love 'em, I let 'em,
When I let 'em, I loose 'em,
    God-damn 'em!

THE MERRY MAID AND THE WICKED MONK

Anonymous

Good father, I have sent for you because
I would not temper with thy holy laws,
And yet, I know that something is amiss,
For when I see the youths and maidens kiss,
I tramble and my very knees grow weak,
Until my chamber I am forced to seek,
And there, with cheeks aflame, in floods of tears,
I toss with strangely mingled hopes and fears.

And father, strange to say, throughout the night,
Although my figure, as you see, is slight,
I dream I have a ripe, voluptuous form,
And strong arms, 'round me, hold me close and warm,
Until at last, I blush to say,
My very garments seem to melt away,
Until, as nature clad me, there I stand,
The willing victim to a wandering hand.

And at these times, when I seem not alone,
The form that holds me is not like my own.
It has not swelling globes here, such as these,
No sloping thighs, nor rounded dimpled knees,
And stranger still—pray, father dear, draw near,
The greatest difference seems to be—just—here.

Dear father, should I pray and fast in pain?
Or sleep and dream those blissful dreams again?
It seems not sin and yet my mirrow shows
A face where shame and deepest color grows.
Tell me it is not wicked, father dear,
To find myself with new sensations, here.
Ah heaven! You burn with fever too, it seems.
Are you, as well, a prey to fitful dreams?

21

And once I dreamed far more than I have told:
This handsome stranger once was overbold,
And I will show thee father, if I may
Just what was done. I could not but obey.
The Sun had set. The stars were in the sky,
And I was trembling, though I knew not why,
And here upon this couch I lay, like this,
When on my lips I felt a burning kiss.

Yes! That is like it! Just the very same!
My arms reached upward. I was not to blame.
For all my soul seemed hungering to feel
The strange delight that made my senses reel.
It seemed so strange that pleasure should be pain,
And yet I fain would suffer, once again.

'Twas thus—and so—and ever did I strain
To meet half way the source of all my pain.
My voice came fitful—broken—just now as now—
I was not mistress of myself I vow!
I clasped the spirit visitor like this—
Through all my veins I felt his maddening kiss.
My pulse went wild—I knew not what was done—
And—goodness gracious! . . . .
. . . . . How that man can run!

MAN, THE HUMAN
Anonymous

Man on top of woman hasn't long to stay—
His head is full of business, and his ass is full of play;
He goes in like a lion, and comes out like a lamb;
Buttons up his pants, and doesn't give a damn!

22

EPIGRAMS FROM PRIAPUS

Selected from Priapeia. 1889

V.

Thought I be wooden Priapus (as thou see'st,)
With wooden sickle and with prickle of wood,
Yet will I seize you, Girl! and hold thee seized;
And This, however gross, withouten fraud,
Stiffer than lyre-string or than twisted rope
I'll thrust and bury to thy seventh rib.

IX.

Why laugh such laughter, O most silly maid?
My form Praxiteles nor Scopas hewed:
To me no Phidian handwork finish gave;
But me a bailiff hacked from shapeless log,
And quoth my maker, "Thou Priapus be!"
Yet on me gazing forthright gigglest thou
And holdeth funny matter to deride
The pillar perking from the groin of me.

XLIV.

What shouldst say this spear (though I'm wooden) be wishing
Whenas a maiden chance me in the middle to kiss.
Here none augur we need: Believe my word she is saying:—
"Let the rude spear in me work with its natural wont!"

LXXXIV.

What news be here? what send those angry Gods?
Whenas in silent night that snow-hued boy
To my warm bosom clasped lay concealed,
Venus was dormant nor in manly guise
My sluggard prickle raised his sluggard head.

Art pleased (Priapus!) under leafy tree
Wont with wine-tendrils sacred sconce to wreathe
And seat thee ruddy with thy ruddled yard?
But, O Tryphallus, oft with freshest flowers
Artlessly garlanded thy brow be crowned
And with loud shouting often drove from thee.
What aged Raven or what agile Daw
Would peck thy holy face with horny beak.
Farewell, Priapus! naught to thee owe I,
Farewell, forsaker damn'd of private parts!
Pale with neglect amid the fields shalt lie
Where savage bandog shall bepiss thee or
Wild boar shall rub thee with his ribs mud-caked.
Accused organ! Oh, by whom my pains
Shall with sore righteous penalty be paid?
Howe'er thou 'plain, no more shall tender boy
Ope to thy bidding, nor on groaning bed
His mobile buttocks writhe with aiding art:
Nor shall the wanton damsel's legier hand
Stroke thee, or rub on thee her lubric thigh.
A two-fanged mistress, Romulus old remembering,
Awaits thee; middlemost whose sable groin
And hide time-loosened thou with coynte-rime bewrayed
And hung in cobwebs fain shalt block the way.
Such prize is thine who thrice and four times shalt
Engulf thy lecherous head in fosse profound.
Though slick or languid lie thou, still thou must
Rasp her 'til wretched, wretched thou shalt fill
Thrice or e'en fourfold times her cavernous gape;
And naught this haughty sprite shall 'vail thee when
Plunging thine errant head in plashing mire.
Why lies it lazy? Doth its sloth displease thee?
For once thou mayest weaken it unavenged;
But when that golden boy again shall come,
Soon as his patter on the path shall hear,

LXXXIV. *Continued.*

Grant that a restless swelling rouse my nerve
Lustful a-sudden and upraise it high,
Nor cease excite it and excite it more
'Til wanton Venus burst my weaked side.

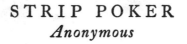

STRIP POKER
Anonymous

Betty and Billy, myself and fair Milly,
    Once sat in a strip-poker game.
All of us truly were young and unruly,
    But the *pep* it was there just the same.

The cards that I had were running quite bad,
    Then suddenly, they came to me great:
From out of the slush, I cornered a flush
    Of diamonds, the four to the eight.

Betty and Billy dropped out, leaving Milly
    And yours very truly to fight it alone:
I raised it a tie and, flicker me eye,
    She saw it and raised it a *comb*.

This kinda hurt, I saw with my *shirt,*
    With a *coat* I raised in great haste.
She looked with her belt and, "Oi gevelt!"
    Boosted it high with her *waist.*

But I didn't flinch, it sure was a cinch,
    So I bet every stitch that I had.
She saw, if you please, with her *silken chemise*
    And—(stopped by the censors)—too bad!

ANOTHER PIECE

Anonymous

"Now Bill," she said, "No more tonight,
  For three you've had already."
She was indeed quite liberal,
  But then, he was her steady.

"But," Bill replied with great emotion,
  "Can't you see, dear, that I crave it,
And, furthermore, what is the use
  In endeavoring to save it?"

"Learn to control yourself," she said,
  "For soon we will be married;
Accomplish this, and happy we'll be."
  This was how she parried.

"But it's ripe, my little angel girl,
  And will not last forever."
She smiled, and answered tauntingly,
  "Now, don't you think you're clever?"

"Oh my love," he said, "another piece,
  I'll have it stripped, my dear;
One more will hurt neither you nor me
  So banish your unfounded fear."

"Well here," she said, "you may have it,
  But you must strip it yourself."
He slowly stripped the herbacious fruit
  And ate the whole thing himself.

THE PIONEERS
Anonymous

The pioneers have hairy ears,
 They piss through leather britches;
They wipe their ass on broken glass
 Those hardy sons-of-bitches!

When cunt is rare they fuck a bear,
 They knife him if he snitches;
They knock their cocks against the rocks,
 Those hardy sons-of-bitches!

They take their ass upon the grass,
 From fairies or from witches;
Their two-pound dinks are full of kinks,
 Those hardy sons-of-bitches!

Without remorse they fuck a horse,
 And beat him if he twitches;
Their mighty dicks are full of nicks,
 Those hardy sons-of-bitches!

To make a mule stand for the tool,
 He's beat with hickory switches;
They use their pricks for walking sticks,
 Those hardy sons-of-bitches!

Great joy they reap from buggering sheep
 In sundry bogs and ditches;
Nor give a damn if it be a ram—
 Those hardy sons-of-bitches!

When booze is rare they do not care,
 They take a shot of *Fitches;**
They fuck their wives with butcher knives,
 Those hardy sons-of-bitches!

* Fitches' hair tonic.

THE DIABETIC DOG
Anonymous

A farmer's dog came into town,
   His christian name was Runt.
A noble pedigree had he,
   Noblesse oblige his stunt.

And as he trotted down the street,
   'Twas beautiful to see
His work at every corner and
   His work at every tree.

He watered every gateway too
   And never missed a post,
For piddling was his specialty,
   And piddling was his boast.

They city curs looked on amazed
   With deep and jealous rage,
To see a simple country dog
   The piddler of the age.

Then all the dogs from everywhere,
   Were summoned by a yell
To sniff the country stranger o'er,
   And judge him by his small.

Some thought that he a king might be,
   Beneath his tail a rose,
So every city dog drew nigh
   And sniffed it up his nose.

They smelled him over one by one,
   They smelled him two by two,
And noble Runt, in high disdain,
   Stood still 'til they were through.

Then just to show the whole shebang
  He didn't care a dam',
He trotted to a grocery store
  And piddled on a ham.

He piddled in a mackerel keg,
  He piddled on the floor,
And when the grocer kicked him out,
  He piddled through the door.

Behind him all the city dogs
  Lined up with instinct true,
To start a piddling carnival
  And see the stranger through.

They showed him every piddling post
  They had in all the town,
And started in, with many a wink,
  To pee the stranger down.

They sent for champion piddlers who
  Were always on the go,
Who sometimes did a piddling stunt
  Or gave a piddling show.

They sprung these on him suddenly
  When midway in the town,
Runt only smiled, and polished off
  The ablest, white and brown.

For Runt was with them every trick,
  With vigor and with vim,
A thousand piddlers more or less
  Were all the same to him.

So he was wetting merrily,
  With hind legs kicking high,
When most were hoisting legs in bluff,
  And piddling mighty dry.

Then on and on Runt sought new grounds,
  By piles of scrap and rust,
'Til every city dog went dry
  And only piddled dust.

But ever on went noble Runt
  As wet as any rill,
And all the champion city pups
  Were peed to a standstill.

Then Runt did freehand piddling,
  With fancy fiisrt and fiings,
Like *double drip* and *gimlet twist,*
  And all that sort of thing.

And all the time this country dog
  Did never wink nor grin,
But piddled blithely out of town
  As he came piddling in.

Envoi:
The city dogs convention held,
  To ask, "what did defeat us?"
But no one ever put them wise
  That Runt had diabetes.

———

THRILLS AND SHOCKS

Anonymous

You may get thrills and shocks
  In many different ways,
But the dif' 'tween thrills and shocks
  Is but twenty-eight short days.

THE KHAN OF KUSPIDOR

Anonymous

In India, in royal state,
Dwelt an illustrious potentate.
  When he would pass, the throngs would roar,
  "Behold the Khan of Kuspidor!"
With mighty chest and skin of yellow,
He was a most imposing fellow;
  And when, in his regalia dressed,
  Diamonds and rubies spanned his chest.
To care for his domestic duties
He kept a thousand brunette beauties,
  Who swarmed around his royal knees,
  Living a life of royal ease.
It kept his massive bollocks busy
Running the gamut from Maud to Lizzie,
  And when he took his royal pleasure
  The juice would fill a gallon measure.
The mass of hard-on that he carried
He'd plunge in every puss he married,
  Or, to the horror of his harem,
  He'd wave it at 'em just to scare 'em.
Tho strong and valorous in his might,
The Khan would rather frig than fight—
  His dames acclaimed with one accord,
  "The prick is mightier than the sword!"
Each night the Khan would hit his bed
He'd have a fresh-trapped maidenhead,
  Which, after fondling with his finger,
  He'd finish with his hairy stinger.
No dusky damsel dodged his wiles:
He could smell a cunt a thousand miles.
  Sometimes the Khan would play the fool
  And let a lady lip his tool,
But, "after all," he used to say,
"I like the good old fashioned way."

But time went on, the story said,
　　And rebellion reared its horrid head:
And all of the people to a man
Went out one night and rushed the Khan.
　　And now those people bow no more
　　Unto the Khan of Kuspidor.
'Tis said he's way down deep in Hades,
Running his red-hot tool in ladies!

LITTLE LESSONS

Anonymous

"Oh! You have touched me—deeply—"
　　The young thing whispered low.
He pleaded: "Come! Oh, come with me!"
　　She could not answer, "No."
She said, "I'll be your pupil."
　　And added softly then,
"I may as well learn things from you
　　As to learn from other men."

They dined alone that evening,
　　And the young man got his wish.
They even broke the unwritten law
　　Of *nevaire before ze feesh.*
At half-past three next morning
　　He staggered home again,
She had taught him tricks he never knew,
　　That she'd learned from other men!

STACKOLEE

Anonymous

Stackolee was a good man:
Everybody he did love.
The pimps and whores all swore by Stack—
By the everlasting stars above
   They all loved Stackolee!

What do you know about this—
What in 'ell do you know about that:
He killed old Billy Lyons
Over a damned old Stetson hat—
   Poor old Stackolee!

They took him to the jail-house
And threw his ass in a cell.
All the whores and pimps went down
To bid poor Stack farewell—
   Poor old Stackolee!

Judge Murphy rose for sentence;
His eyes were filled with tears.
He said. "I won't be hard on you, Stack,
I'll just give you ninety-nine years."
   Poor old Stackolee!

Stack's girl was a good girl;
She was just as true as steel.
She said, "I'll get the dough for Stack,
On him I'll never squeal."
   Poor old Stackolee!

She hustled in the morning,
She hustled in the night;
She got so thin from hustling
She was an awful sight.
    She'd get the dough for Stackolee!

One night it rained like hell;
She had an awful time.
She said, "I won't break Stacko's luck."
She shook her fannie for a dime
    Getting the dough for Stackolee!

She got a nice clean crib
Down behind the jail.
She hung a sign upon her door,
"Fresh fish here for sale."
    She'd get the dough for Stackolee!

Another night she had bad luck:
She got an old nigger who gave her a buck;
She said, "You know I've got no change,
So give yourself another fuck
    For poor old Stackolee!"

One night came a wireless
And everybody sighed;
It said that at 8:45
The poor old pimp had died.
    Means a funeral for Stackolee!

When old Stack's girl
Heard this awful news,
She was seated at her bedside
Pulling on her shoes;
    Having the blues for Stackolee!

They had a rubber-tired hearse
And had some rubber-tired hacks.
After that came a procession
Of about ten thousand macks.
   Off to the grave of Stackolee!

When they got to the graveyard
And saw that awful hole,
Those pimps and whores fell on their knees
And asked the Lord to save their souls.
   Beside the grave of Stackolee!

I never heard so much talk,
I never heard so much gab.
One pimp pulled out a needle,
In his arm he took a jab.
   Beside the grave of Stackolee!

Another pimp's yen came on him;
I thought, by God, he'd choke—
He pulled out his bamboo, lit his lamp,
And laid on his hip to smoke.
   Beside the grave of Stackolee!

An itchy-nosed pimp stepped out—
Said, "Folks, I ain't got much to say,"
Pulled out a bindle and took a bang,
Said, "Goodbye Doctor Gray."
   At the grave of Stackolee!

And now he's gone, why, let him go;
Poor Stack is now in his last hole;
And all the whores and pimps they say
"May the Lord have mercy on his soul."
   —And that's the last of Stackolee!

LOVE'S POWER
Anonymous

"O Sir," quoth the pretty maid,
　"Let me know what 'tis you would have?
For you need not at all be afraid,
　I will grant what in reason you crave:
For I ne'er in my life would deny
　What a man did in justice require;
But you and I soon shall comply,
　And I'll warrant I'll quench thy love's fire."

"If thou art so earnest do dally,
　Come make use of time while you may,
Thy skill I will not undervalue,
　Then prithee, Love, let's to the play:
Methinks thou art somewhat too devious;
　'Tis time we should have been nigher,
To linger it seems to be grevious,
　I'll warrant I'll quench thy love's fire."

The young man supposing her greedy
　Fell eagerly into the sport,
He found she was wanting and needy,
　And needless it was for to court.
But as they were hugging together,
　She cried, "O come nigher and nigher."
His heart was as light as a feather,
　And he had both his wish and desire.
The damsel was mightily pleased,
　And kissed him a thousand times o'er,
Quoth she, "Now my sorrows are eased,
　But I must have a little touch more:
O, lie down for a while to rest thee,
　That I may enjoy my desire;
I hope that the fates they will bless thee;
　I quench, but thou kindlest my fire."

No longer he stood there delaying,
    But stoutly he fell to it again,
Where he gave a prod at their playing
    The damsel returned him ten;
For she grew more eager and eager,
    Her eyes they did sparkle like fire,
Quoth he, "I do own I am the weaker,
    But still I enjoy my desire."

The young man began for to tire
    And his cudgel began to lay down,
Which made the young damsel admire
    And straight she began for to frown:
Quoth he, "I have done what is fit,
    No reason can more require;"
But her brows upon her then she knit,
    And still she did want her desire.

*SWEET AND PRETTY LITTLE NOSE

Anonymous

Oh, sweet and pretty little nose, so charming unto me;
Oh, were I but the sweetest rose, I'd give my scent to thee.
Oh, make it full and honey sweet, that I may such it all;
T'would be for me the greatest treat, a real festival.
How sweet and how nutritious your darling nose does seem;
It would be more delicious than strawberries and cream!

*This is the acme of rottenness—with, however, a Pathological explanation. It occurs on page 225 of Kraft-Ebbing's Psychopathia Sexualis (XII edition, The Rebman Co., New York) referring to body-fetichism, and nose-fetichism in particular. Kraft-Ebbing gives it as coming to him from England.

*THE CHISHOLM TRAIL

A Cowboy Song

Now get 'round boys and listen to my tale,
And learn my troubles on the Chisholm Trail;

Come a ti yi yippy, come a ti yi yay,
Come a ti yi yippy, yippy yay!

Left Texas on October twenty-third
And travelled up the trail with he 2 U herd;

Chorus:

With saddled ass and pony on the lope,
I am the best man who ever throwed a rope.

Chorus:

On a ten dollar horse and a forty dollar saddle
Comes I from Texas with the long-horn cattle.

Chorus:

The boys found a stray and the boss said, "Kill it,"
So I shot him in the ass with the end of a skillet.

Chorus:

Always afore I sleep the moon shines bright,
And I am up in the mornin' 'afore daylight.

Chorus:

It's cloudy in the West and looks like rain,
And my god-damn slicker's in the wagon again.

My name is Bill Taylor and my love's a squaw,
Who lives on the banks of the muddy Wichita.

Chorus:

I asked for tail and I handed her a quarter;
Says she, "Young man, I'm a cowpuncher's daughter."

Chorus:

So out comes a dollar to fill her greasy hand;
Says she, "Young man, will your old dingwallace stand?"

Chorus:

I grabbed her then and throwed her on the grass,
My toe-holt slipped and I rammed it up her ass.

Chorus:

I fucked her standin' and I fucked her lyin'
And if she'd had some wings I'd a fucked her flyin'.

Chorus:

Says she, "Young man, you're nothin' but a kid"—
Says she, "You'll remember me." And, b'God, I did.

Chorus:

'Bout nine days on my prick began to swell,
And I wisht that squaw in the lowest pits o' hell.

Chorus:

I weent to the big boss for to draw my roll,
And he had figured me nine dollars in the hole.

Chorus:

So I sold old Baldy and hung up the saddle,
And then I bid farewell to the god-damn cattle.

Chorus:

*The Chisholm Trail was named for Jesse Chisholm, a hal
breed Indian, who piloted the first herd of long-horns fror
Texas to the then newly completed U. P. railroad in Wester
Kansas.   Dodge City was the northern terminus of the roa
and for several years enormous herds of cattle were trailed u
from Texas to be shipped to Eastern markets.

* The Chisholm Trail was named for Jesse Chisholm, a half-breed Indian,
who piloted the first herd of long-horns from Texas to the then newly completed U. P. railroad in Western Kansas. Dodge City was the northern
terminus of the road and for several years enormous herds of cattle were
trailed up from Texas to be shipped to Eastern markets.

WHAT MY WIFE WANTS TONIGHT
Anonymous

I wonder what my wife will want tonight;
Wonder if the wife will fuss and fight?
I wonder can she tell
That I've been raising hell;
Wonder if she'll know that I've been tight?
My wife is just as nice as nice can be,
I hope she doesn't feel too nice toward me;
For an afternoon of joy
Is hell on the old boy.
I wonder what the wife will want tonight!

HOOKSHOP KATE
Anonymous

Did you ever hear of the grewsome fate
  That befell the heroine Hookshop Kate?
Though now she has passed to the Great Beyond
  She once was the queen of the demi-monde.
She was not so handsome as looks go,
  But when it came to jazzing that gal could go;
And the one pet brag of Hookshop Kate
  Was that she'd never met her mate.

When the gold stampede caused a restless much,
  Hookshop Kate got in the rush;
She cast all civilized tools adrift,
  For she heard that cocks in the North froze stiff,
And figured that guys with frozen pep
  Would never have to watch their step.
For conventional methods were out of date
  In a frigging match with Hookshop Kate.

She landed in Fairbanks one winter's night,
  And issued her challenge to all in sight;
And all the miners who tested her power
  Were frigged to a whisper inside of an hour.
And the records show, before Spring came,
  That every man in town was lame;
For not one could travel the gait
  That was set by amorous Hookshop Kate.

With an air of contempt she sallied forth
  And bade farewell to the frozen North.
She headed straight for Hawaii's Isles,
  Where men were decked in Nature's smiles;
Hoping in vain that the naked truth
  Would show her a man with pep and youth.
But alas! she was doomed to the same sad fate,
  For none was the equal of Hookshop Kate.

41

Then the Hawaiians placed her on a throne,
  And crowned here queen of the Frigging Zone,
Where she reigned supreme for two short years,
  But one morning her subjects found her in tears.
When they asked the cause she only sighed,
  And they knew she longed to be satisfied;
So they resolved to find her a mate
  Who could crimp the back of Hookshop Kate.

They inserted a luring, sensuous *ad*
  In the Woman's Monthly, and it had
A very wondrous quick effect
  In bringing news of things erect:
A bookseller came upon the scene
  And asked to be ushered to the queen;
For he claimed he knew of a potentate,
  Who could outfrig great Hookshop Kate

'Twas a sheep-herder from a distant Isle,
  Who had never been tempted by woman's wile;
But had spent his life with his wandering flock,
  Developing by hand his phenomenal cock.
'Twas a daily thing for him, they said,
  To frig sixty sheep ere he went to bed.
When this happy data reached Hookshop Kate
  She sent for this sheepish potentate.

The bookseller found him flat on a rock
  Breaking cocoanuts with his muscular cock,
And he laughed up his sleeve as he placed a bet
  On the frigging that Hookshop Kate would get.
He convinced the herder that frigging sheep
  Was an action base, profane and cheap;
As a bookseller will, he proved that fate
  Had called him to satisfy Hookshop Kate.

When they arrived on Hawaii's shore,
    The town was bedecked as never before;
And the band was playing to welcome them in,
    And all was in readiness to begin.
The herder and bookseller lead the parade,
    Followed by virgins and Redlight Jade,
And the whole procession marched in state
    To the very door of Hookshop Kate.

The fray was scheduled for ten o'clock.
    Meanwhile the sheep-herder tuned up his jock
By trying it out on a dozen of dames,
    Who acknowledged that he was a bundle of flames.
As the hour drew near the betting was great—
    The number of times would be marked on a slate—
'Twas a frig to a finish without a wait,
    Much to the delight of Hookshop Kate.

When the clock struck ten came a breathless pause—
    The sheep-herder entered 'mid great applause—
In front, his pants stuck out two feet
    In anticipation of one real treat;
While in the chamber with curtains drawn
    Was Hookshop Kate just egging him on—
Outside, the crowd decided to wait
    And see what would happen to Hookshop Kate.

Outside, that night, the vigil was kept,
    And not a single eye had slept;
And the moans and groans and grunts inside
    Swayed the throng like an ebbing tide.
They all left marks of their butts behind,
    And not one dry spot could you find—
But all sat tight to learn the fate
    Of her frigging highness Hookshop Kate.

Next morning the bookseller came with the key
    To decide what the herder's fate should be.
He found the slate, as he felt in the dark—
    Passed it out to the crowd to examine the mark—
They counted a hundred and sixty or more.
    Then the bookseller threw wide open the door—
When the lights went on, to their surprise
    This is the sight that met their eyes:

With a happy smile, propped up in bed,
    The famous Hookshop Kate was dead.
While under the bed the sheep-herder guy
    Jacked off at the post without batting an eye:
And he murmured, at each violent jerk,
    And in intervals between each squirt,
"All your Hookshop cunt you can keep
    If you hurry me back to my lovely sheep."

A PASTORAL

Anonymous

The sheep-herder lay in the tall, tall grass,
And his favorite dog lay close to his ass.
Through a hole in his worn blue overalls
A toothless ewe was licking his balls.
A magpie sat on the fence close by
And gazed on the scene with a watchful eye—
His gun went off—and the old ewe quit—
The hound dog yelped—and the magpie shit!

THE BASTARD KING OF ENGLAND

RUDYARD KIPLING

Oh, the bards they sing of an English King
　　Who lived long years ago;
And he ruled his land with an iron hand,
　　But his mind was weak and low.
He was used to hunt the royal stag
　　Within his royal wood,
But 'twas none but knew that his greatest sport
　　Was pulling his royal pud.

And his nether garb was a woolen shirt
　　Which used to hide his hide;
But this undershirt couldn't hide the dirt
　　That no one could abide.
He was wild and wooly and full of fleas
　　That humans ne'er could stand;
And his terrible dong to his knees hung down—
　　The Bastard King of England!

Now the Queen of Spain was an amorous dame,
　　A sprightly dame was she,
And she longed to fool with his Majesty's tool
　　So far across the sea.
So she sent a note to the dirty King
　　By her royal messenger,
And requested his Majesty's sailing to Spain
　　To spend a month with her.

But when Philip of France got the news one day,
　　He turned to all his court
And he said, "My fair Queen prefers this clown
　　Because my tool is short."
So he sends abroad Marquis Siphylissap,
　　Who smacked of *fairyland,*
To supply the Queen with a dose of clap
　　To trap our Dear Old England.

45

Then the news of this filthy deed was heard
    In Windsor's merry halls,
And the King did swear he would have anon
    The Frenchman's greasy balls.
So he offered the half of all his lands,
    And the whole of Queen Hortense,
To the trusty lord of his English court
    Who'd nut the King of France.

So the loyal Duke of Essexshire
    Betook himself to France;
When he swore he was a fruiter the King
    Took down his royal pants:
Then around his prong he tied a thong
    And gaily galloped along
'Til at last in Windsor's merry halls,
    Was the Frenchman and his dong.

And the King threw up, and he shit his pants;
    For in the lengthy ride
The thong had stretched by a yard or more
    The fucking Frenchman's pride.
And then all the ladies of London town
    Who saw the mighty *stand*
Cried aloud, "To hell with the English Crown,"
    And made Philip King of England.

~

HIS ONLY LIMITATION
Anonymous

My cock has been in many cunts,
But in never more than one at once!

A REHEARSAL

Anonymous

I'm thinking of the rainy night—
  The rest had hurried home—
And we, in Deacon Foster's pew,
  Were sitting all alone;
You were a seeker then, dear Will,
  But not of things above—
The length, the depth, the breadth, the height
  Of everlasting love—

Oh! What sweet words of love you spoke,
  And kissed away each tear;
And how I trembled at the thought
  Lest someone should appear;
But when you turned the lights all out,
  To guard against surprise,
I bade farewell to every fear
  And wiped my weeping eyes.

Ithought, could I these doubts remove,
  These gloomy doubts that rise,
And see the Canaan that we love
  With unbeclouded eyes!
And as you climbed the pulpit stairs,
  And viewed the landscape o'er,
Not Jordan's stream, nor Death's cold flood
Could fright us from the floor.

And when you fixed the cushions up,
  And I reclined at ease,
The pulpit pillow 'neath my head,
  And you on bended knees;
With your warm kisses on my lips,
  How could I stay your hand;
The veil wsa lifted, and by faith
  You viewed the promised land.

And Oh, what rapturous feelings
  Thrilled every nerve, and when
I cried, *Oh Lord, my heart is touched,*
  You shouted out, *Amen!*
My very soul was all ablaze,
  I thought that I could see
The land of rest, the saint's delight,
  The heaven prepared for me.

I thought, *a charge to keep I have*
  With mingled fear and shame;
How anxiously I watched, dear Will,
  'Til I came 'round again!
In my distress I vainly strove
  To check the welling tears.
The precious blood poured freely forth
  And conquered all my fears.

But that was many years ago,
  And I've no doubt that you
Remember still the rainy night
  In Deacon Foster's pew!
But Oh, my first experience
  Will ne'er forgotten be
While dow nthe stream of life we glide
  To our eternity.

POOR WHITE TRASH

Anonymous

The rich man uses vaseline,
  The poor man uses lard,
The nigger uses axle grease
  But he gets it twice as hard!

FRANKIE AND JOHNNIE

Anonymous

Frankie and Johnnie were lovers:
  Goodness, Oh God! How they'd love—
Swore to be true to each other,
  True as the stars above.
For he was her man,
  But he done her wrong!

Frankie was a good girl,
  Most everybody knows,
She gave a hundred dollars
  To Johnnie for a suit of clothes.
Cause he was her man,
  But he done her wrong!

Frankie worked in a crib-joint,
  A place that's got two doors;
Gave all her money to Johnnie,
  Who spent it on parlor-house whores.
God-damn his soul,
  He done her wrong!

Frankie was a fucky hussy—
  That's what all the pricks said—
And they kept her so damn busy,
  She never had time to get out of bed.
But he done her wrong,
God-damn his soul,

Frankie hung a sign on her door,
  "No more fish for sale."
Then she went looking for Johnnie
  To give him all her kale.
He was a-doin' her wrong,
God-damn his soul,

49

Frankie went down Fourth Street
    To get a glass of steam-beer;
Said to the man called bartender,
    "Has my lovin' Johnnie been here?
God-damn his soul,
    He's a-doin' me wrong!"

"I couldn't tell you no story,
    I couldn't tell you no lie,
I saw your Johnnie an hour ago
    With a coon called Alice Bly.
God-damn his soul,
    He was a-doin' you wrong!"

Frankie ran back to the crib-joint,
    Took the oilcloth off the bed,
Took out a bindle of coke
    And snuffed it right up in her head;
God-damn his soul
    He was a-doin' her wrong!

Then she put on her red kimona,
    This time it wasn't for fun;
Cause right underneath it
    Was a great big forty-four gun.
She went huntin' her man,
    Who was a-doin' her wrong!

She ran along Fish Alley,
    And looked in a window high,
And she saw her lovin' Johnnie
    Finger-frigging Alice Bly.
He was a-doin' her wrong,
    God-damn his soul!

Frankie went to the hop-joint,
   Frankie rang the hop-joint bell:
"Stand back you pimps and whores,
   Or I'll blow you straight to hell.
I'm huntin' my man,
   Who's a-doin' me wrong!"

Frankie ran up the stairway—
   Johnnie hollered, "Please don't shoot!"
But Frankie raised the forty-four
   And went five times, root-ti-toot.
She shot her man,
   'Cause he done her wrong!

"Turn me over Frankie,
   Turn me over slow;
A bullet got me on my right side,
   Oh Gawd! It hurts me so.
You've killed your man,
   But I done you wrong!"

Then came the scene in the courthouse:
   Frankie said, as bold as brass,
"Judge, I didn't shoot him in the third degree,
   I shot him in his big fat ass;
'Cause he was my man,
   An' was a-doin' me wrong!"

Bring out your rubber-tired hearse.
   Bring out your rubber-tired hacks.
Hearse to take Johnnie to the cemetery;
   Hacks to bring all the whores back:
For he's dead and gone,
   'Cause he done her wrong!

They brought a rubber-tired hearse,
  And brought out rubber-tired hacks:
Thirteen pimps went to the cemetery
  But only twelve came back.
He's dead and gone,
  He was a-doin' her wrong!

The sergeant said to Frankie,
  "It may all be for the best,
He always chased 'round parlor-house whores,
  He sure was an awful pest;
Now he's dead and gone,
  He was a-doin' her wrong!"

Three little pieces of crepe
  Hanging on the crib-joint door,
Signifies that Johnnie
  Will never be a pimp no more.
God-damn his soul,
  He done her wrong!

———

JIM TAYLOR

Anonymous

My name is Jim Taylor,
My cock is a whaler,
My bollocks weigh ninety-four pound;

And when I fuck Anna
I fuck 'er God-damn 'er,—
I drive her ass into the ground.

A FOOL THERE WAS
Apologies to Kipling

A fool there was and he met a belle,
  Even as you and I;
  Even as you and I;
And he took her to a swell hotel,
  Even as you and I;
And he thought himself a smart young gink
As he wrote *and wife* with the pen and ink,
And slyly gave the clerk a wink;
  Even as you and I.

They went up the hallway and into the room,
  Even as you and I;
Trying their best to look bride and groom,
  Even as you and I;
She was Frisco's most beautiful belle,
And the fool was all set to give her hell,
But when you're past forty you never can tell.
  Even as you and I.

She took off her shirtwaist and showed her white breast,
  Even as you and I;
And he stripped right down to the hair on his chest,
  Even as you and I;
They jumped into bed, his brain was a-fire,
He was anxious as hell and mad with desire,
When he suddenly discovered he had a flat tire,
  Even as you and I.

The Fool sat up and he made a prayer,
  Even as you and I;
To a rag and a bone and a hank of hair,
And for once in his life he prayed on the square;
But the beautiful maid gave up in despair,
She sent for a chink, gave the fool the air—
  Even as you and I.

53

THE BALLAD OF YUKON JAKE

TED PARMENTIER

Oh, the North Countree is a hard countree
   That mothers a bloody brood;
And its icy arms hold hidden charms
   For the greedy, the sinful and lewd,
And strong men rust from the gold and lust
   That sears the Northland's soul;
But the wickedest born, from the Pole to the **Horn,**
   Is the Hermit of Sharktooth Shoal.

Now Jacob Kaime was the Hermit's name,
   In the days of his pious youth,
Ere he cast a smirch on the Baptist Church
   By betraying a girl named Ruth.
But now men quake at Yukon Jake,
   The Hermit of Sharktooth Shoal;
For that is the name that Jacob Kaime
   Is known by from Nome to the Pole;
He was just a boy and the parson's joy
   Ere he fell for the gold and the muck,
And he learned to pray 'mid the hogs and **hay**
   On a farm near Keokuk.

But a service tale of illicit kale—
   And whiskey and women wild,
Drained the morals clean as a soup tureen
   From this poor but honest child.
He longed for the bite of a Yukon night
   And the Northern-lights' weird flicker,
Or a game of stud in the frozen mud
   And the taste of raw red likker.
He wanted to mush along in the slush,
   With a team of huskie hounds,
And to fire his gat at a beaver hat,
   And knock it out of bounds.

So he left his home for the hell-town Nome,
  On Alaska's ice-ribbed shores,
And he learned to curse and drink, and worse,
  'Til the rum dripped from his pores;
When the boys on a spree were drinking it free
  Ina Malamute saloon,
And Dan McGrew and his dangerous crew
  Shot craps with a piebald coon;
While the kid on his stool banged away like a fool
  At a jag-time melody,
And the barkeep vowed to the hardboiled crowd
  That he'd cremate Sam McGee;

Then Jacob Kaime, who had taken the name
  Of Yukon Jake the Killer,
Would rake the dive with his forty-five
  'Til the atmosphere grew chiller;
With a sharp command he'd make 'em stand
  And deliver their hard earned dust;
Then drink the bar dry of rum and rye,
  As a Klondike bully must;
Without coming to blows he would tweak the nose
  Of Dangerous Dan McGrew,
And, becoming bolder, throw over his shoulder
  The lady that's known as Lou.

Oh, tough as a steak was Yukon Jake,
  Hardboiled as a picnic egg;
He washed his shirt in Klondike dirt,
  And drank his rum by the keg.
In fear of their lives, or because of their wives,
  He was shunned by the best of his pals;
And outcast he, from the cameraderie
  Of all but wild animals.
So he bought him the whole of Sharktooth Shoal,
  A reef in the Bering Sea,
Where he lived by himself on a sea-lion's shelf
  In lonely iniquity.

But miles away, in Keokuk,
    Did a lovely maiden fight
To remove the smirch from the Baptist Church
    By bringing the heathen light;
And the elders declared that all would be squared
    If she carried the Holy Words
From her Keokuk home to the hell-hole Nome
    And save those awful birds.
So two weeks later she took a freighter
    For the gold-cursed land near the Pole,
Blut heaven ain't made for a girl that's betrayed,
    She was wrecked on Sharktooth Shoal!

All hands were tossed in the sea and lost,
    All but the maiden Ruth,
Who swam to the edge of the sea-lion's ledge
    Where abode the love of her youth.
He was hunting a seal for his evening meal
    (He handled a mean harpoon)
When he saw at his feet not something to eat,
    But a girl in a frozen swoon;
He dragged her to his lair by the frozen hair,
    And he rubbed her knees with gin—
To his great surprise she opened her eyes,
    And revealed—his original sin!

His eight months' beard grew still and weird,
    And it felt like a chestnut burr;
He swore by his gizzard and the Arctic blizard,
    That he'd do right by her.
The cold sweat froze on the end of his nose,
    'Til it gleamed like a Teckla pearl,
While her bright hair fell like a flame from hell
    Down the back of the grateful girl.

56

But a hopeless rake was Yukon Jake,
  The Hermit of Sharktooth Shoal;
And the dizzy maid he re-betrayed,
  And wrecked her immortal soul!
Then he rowed her ashore with a broken oar,
  And he sold her to Dan McGrew
For a huskie dog and a hot egg-nog,
  As rascals are wont to do.

Now ruthless Ruth is a maid uncouth
  With scarlet cheeks and lips,
And she sings rough songs to the drunken throngs
  That come from the sealing ships.
For a rouge-stained kiss from this infamous miss
  They will give a seal's sleek fur,
Or perhaps a sable, if they are able,
  For it's all the same to her.

Oh, the North Countree is a rough countree
  That mothers a bloody brood;
And its icy arms hold hidden charms,
  For the sinful, the greedy and lewd;
And strong men rust with the gold and lust
  That sears the Northland's soul,
But the wickedest born from the Pole to the Horn,
  Is the Hermit of Sharktooth Shoal.

———

HIZZEN AND HERN

Anonymous

Drifting down the stream of izzen,
  They were seated in the stern,
And she had her hand on hizzen,
  And he had his hand on hern.

GOOD MORNING MISTER FISHERMAN
Anonymous

Good morning mister fisherman, I wish you very well,
Good morning mister fisherman, I wish you very well;
Pray tell me have you any sea-crabs for to sell?
    Mush a ding eye, mush a doo eye day!

I have got sea-crabs, one—two—three,
I have got sea-crabs, one—two—three;
So take any that you want for its all the same to me.
    Mush a ding eye, mush a doo eye day!

So I grabbed one by his backbone,
So I grabbed one by his backbone;
And I rustled and I tussled 'til I got the bastard home.
    Mush a ding eye, mush a doo eye day!

When I got home everybody was asleep,
When I got home everybody was asleep;
So I put him in the pisspot there for to keep.
    Mush a ding eye, mush a doo eye day!

The ould woman got up to do a little squat,
The ould woman got up to do a little squat;
And the go-damned sea-crab grabbed her by the twat.
    Mush a ding eye, mush a doo eye day!

Ould man, ould man, what shall I do,
Ould man, ould man, what shall I do?
The divil's in the pisspot and's got me by the flue.
    Mush a ding eye, mush a doo eye day!

So I ran over and lifted up her clothes,
So I ran over and lifted up her clothes;
And he took his other pincher and he grabbed me by the nose
    Mush a ding eye, mush a doo eye day!

Now Johnny, have the doctor hitch up his horse and cart,
Now Johnny, have the doctor hitch up his horse and cart;
To get your father's nose and your mother's arse apart.
    Mush a ding eye, mush a doo eye day!

DON'T LOOK AT ME THAT WAY, STRANGER

Anonymous

Don't look at me that way, stranger—
    I didn't shit in your seat;
I've just come down from the mountains
    And my balls are covered with gleet.

I've been up in the Lehigh Valley—
    Me an' me old pal Lou,
A-pimpin' for a whorehouse,
    And a God-damned fine one, too.

It was there that I first fucked Nellie,
    She was the village belle;
I was only a low-down pander,
    But I loved that girl like Hell!

But along comes a city slicker,
    All handsome and gay and rich,
And he stole away my Nellie,
    The stinkin' son-of-a-bitch!

I'm just restin' my ass a moment,
    And when I'm on my way;
I'll get the runt that swiped my cunt,
    If it takes 'til judgment day!

59

THE SKIN MAN
Anonymous

O some may sing of a surgeon's skill—
  He wields a wicked blade—
While not a few prefer G. U.—
  'Tis not a tidy trade;—
Pure science has her acolytes,
  A brave devoted band,
But I'd rather be a skin-man,
  And with the skin-men stand.

Outside the throat-room's dreadful door,
  The knitting women wait,
While all unseen the guillotine
  Keeps up its ghastly gait;
Like plums upon the dewy grass
  The tender tonsils fall,
But neither they nor adenoids
  Intrigue my thoughts at all.

The skin-man never is aroused,
  As breaks the morning pale,
By vehement parturiant
  Or ailing infants' wail,
Nor is he snatched from Morpheus' arms—
  From some delicious dream—
To aid an old prostatic case
  Who cannot start his stream.

Behind his broad expansive desk,
  Mayhap of tropic teak,
He views the rash and takes the cash
  And does it week on week;
His mind is calm, his spirits blithe,
  His future is assured.
  They're never quickly cured.

With ointments bland he tries his hand
　　To soothe, but, ere too late,
If soothing makes them worse again,
　　Then he can stimulate;
If stimulation aggravates,
　　His course runs ever smooth,
For he can cease to stimulate
　　And start once more to soothe.

No paladin of Arthur's age,
　　No gleaming, crested knight
Of old romance, had such a chance
　　His lady to delight;
For him that blush of damask rose,
　　For him that downcast eye,
Who drives the ringworm from her cheek,
　　The itchmite from her thigh.

The lady fine,—the concubine,
　　The virgin and the priest
Discard their pants in bacchic dance
　　From lieus now released;
Tabetic and paretic
　　In corybanic maze,
Surround the guy that got them by
　　And raise their songs of praise.

So farewell dematitis,
　　From you forever free,
Goodbye the bugs that bite us,
　　The louse, the tick, the flea.
Edema and erythema,
　　Pruritis-ani too,
Like driven snow from head to toe,
　　We bid you all adieu.

THE SHIP'S IN THE HARBOR

Anonymous

Oh, the ship's in the harbor,
 She lies by the dock,
Like a young girl and a young man
 With a stiff standing—

—haul away for the mainsail,
 The main-top-set-sail,
Haul away for the mainsail,
 The main-top-set-sail.

And there was young Johnny,
 The pride of her crew,
Who liked to drink whiskey
 And also to—

—water the garden when
 He was at home,
Water the garden when
 He was at home.

He could dive like a diver,
 He could swim like a duck,
He could show the young ladies
 A new way to—

—save their sweet lives if
 A cramp they should take,
Save their sweet lives if
 A cramp they should take.

But alas, we put it in at
 A far Northern port,
And he froze it in chasing
 And broke it off—

—half way to Juneau,
  And half way to Nome,
Half way to Juneau,
  And half way to Nome.

Oh, the ship's in the harbor,
  She lies by the dock,
But alas for poor Johnny,
  He has no more—
—yardarm to splice with,
  Or topmast to brace,
Yardarm to splice with,
  Or topmast to brace.

BERKELEY

Anonymous

O, Harvard is run by Princeton,
  And Princeton is run by Yale,
And Yale is run by Vassar,
  And Vassar's run by tail;
But Stanford's run by stud-horse juice,
  They say its made by hand,
It's the house of clap and syph,
  It's the asshole of the land.

THE FALL OF MAN

Anonymous

So beautiful the earth, in Nature's eyes,
A soul was sent to dwell, in human guise,
A form of God-like beauty and of might,
To drink the sunshine and to dream at night.

Strange visions came to Nature's first child, Man:
In those old days, when first the world began,
Unclad and lone he roved from spot to spot
And longed and yearned for something which was not.

Until, at last, a prayer went up to heaven
And Nature's noblest gift to man was given:
A gentle, throbbing, trembling, beauteous maid,
Fair as a man, but with a softer shade,
Endowed with beauty and a thousand charms
That sought the sheltering clasp of loving arms.

As children play, in childhood's happy hours,
They romped and played among the sylvan bowers,
Or sported in the streams whose waters sweet
Ran cool beneath the trees at noonday's heat.

And when night's sable banners were unfurled
And darkness wound her arms about the world,
On bed of roses, in some vine-clad nest,
Their drowsy senses found untroubled rest,
And wandering zephers swept across them there,
Unclad, but unashamed, in Eden fair.

No thought had come to them of wild desire
And yet, at times, a smouldering, hidden fire
Seemed slumbering deep within, and fiercer burned.
When, in their sleep, they toward each other turned.

One ambient night of blissful summertime,
A perfect night of Eden's balmy clime,
Eve stretched her languorous limbs in restless sleep
And Adam, at her side, sought slumber deep.

Some trifling thing, perhaps a wind-swayed fern,
A leaf—a bird—caused both of them to turn.
Eve's rounded arm was thrown above her head,
Her dimpled knee just lifted from her bed,
When, by chance, this trifle, light as air,
Their warm lips met and, trembling, lingered there.

They slept no more from dusk to rosy dawn,
'Mongst roses red or on some grassy lawn,
But wakened often, from strange dreams of bliss,
To find their mouths all melting in a kiss.
Their hearts were filled with vague, unknown desire,
Nor knew they to quench this wondrous fire.

A wild unrest upon them settled down
And Adam's brow would often wear a frown,
And then again, he'd stroke her glorious hair,
And gaze into her eyes and call her fair,
Then clasp her fiercely, with encircling arm,
As though to shield her from impending harm;
Then wildly kiss her—eyes—mouth—neck and breast,
While she against him, tightly, closely press't.
Still waited, hungered, starved for something more,
Yet little knew what Nature had in store.
Eve's little, truant, tapering fingers slim,
Beloved of Adam and caressed him,
By accident one night, got wondrous wise,
And found just where the trees of knowledge rise.
Amazed, surprised, confounded, if you please,
But, womanlike, inclined a bit to tease,
She tried experiments of many a kind,
To learn by which she most delight could find.

And Adam, dizzy with her new-found charms,
Gave way to every pressure of her arms
And gave her childish innocence full sway,
Nor cared to check her or say her "Nay."

Then suddenly with savage, passionate clasp,
She drew him to her with an eager grasp
And sank exhausted, yet with cheeks aflame,
A-thrill with feelings which she could not name.
And Adam, swept away on seas of bliss,
Poured all his soul in one long, clinging kiss.

'Twas pain, 'twas pleasure, 'twas a joy intense.
It seemed as tho along each quivering sense,
Swift rivulets of fire had found their way
And burned their hearts. They knew not night nor day,
Nor life, nor death, nor aught that mortals know.

Nor dreamed they, even yet, of further joy,
The one swift dream that comes without alloy,
And bends two loving natures into one,
Too sweet to last—that ends ere 'tis begun.

It came to them like lightening from the sky.
Each thought the very hour of death was nigh,
Yet longed to live. Delirious pain
Went sweeping through their inmost souls again
And black oblivion brooded for an hour,
O'er passion's birth in Eden's rosy bower.
They only knew they loved each other so.

And when at last, Eve wakened from her swoon,
The night had fled. The glare of Eden's noon
Sent showers of golden light through waving trees,
And subtle fragrance lingered on the breeze.

Throughout the realm of Eden's joyous bower,
All things that live were happy in that hour,
For, led by sweet desire, example given,
They found on earth, the one foretaste of heaven.

. . . .

And since you must know all there is to know,
Her thirst for knowledge, seeking to know all,
Discovered first the secret of the Fall.
But sought the source of her new-found delight,
Turned pale, grew faint, and trembled at the sight:

The trees of knowledge stood—Ah yes, it stood.
Past tense, you see—and while the past was good,
The present need was great without a doubt
And pretty Eve began to fret and pout.
Swept and sighed and said, "I see it all,
For here was life and there, alas! the Fall."

—

MARY'S LITTLE WATCH

Anonymous

Mary had a little watch,
  She swallowed it one day;
And now she's taking cascarets
  To pass the time away.
But as the time went on and on
The watch refused to pass;
So if you want to know the time
  Just look up Mary's ass.

RING--DANG-DOO

Anonymous

Oh, Ring-dang-doo! Pray what is that,
So soft and warm like a pussy-cat,
So warm and round, and split in two?
   She said it was her Ring-dang-doo.

She took me down into her cellar,
She said I was a damn fine feller,
She fed me wine, and whiskey too,
   And let me play with her Ring-dang-doo

"You God-damned fool," her mother said,
"You've gone and broken your maidenhead;
So pack your trunk, and suit-case too,
   And go to hell with your Ring-dang-doo."

She went down town, became a whore,
Hung up a sign outside her door:
"One dollar down or less, will do,
   To take a crack at my Ring-dang-doo."

They came by twos, they came by fours,
Until at last they came in scores;
But she was glad when they were through,
   For they had ruined her Ring-dang-doo.

And now she lies beneath the sod;
Her soul, they say, is gone to God;
But down in Hell, when Satan's blue,
   He takes a whirl at her Ring-dang-doo.

AN ERROR

E. P. MATHER

Lay she naked in the sea
All the salt would sweetened be.
Showed she in the sunset West
Eastward-praying Christian even
Would look back and think it best
So to gaze and lose his heaven.
I saw her gleaming in the night,
"O Night," I cried in agitation,
"What is this phantom of delight?
Is it a tender ghost which haunts me,
Or a heated virgin wants me
For the joys of copulation?"
As in answer to this riddle,
She put down her hands and sighed,
Clasped the blossom of her middle
With her fingers, and replied:
"Fairest teeth need daily scraping
With an aromatic twig;
Chastest parts will sigh for raping
With a something bold and big.
Massulmen, has this not wrung you?
Is there not a zebb among you?"
Here I felt him crack his joint
While the vehemence which swelled him
Lifted up the clothes which held him
To a noticeable point.
So I let him out, but she
Started back in terror:
"I said twigs, and here's a tree.
Is there not some error?"

CAROLINA: A PARODY

Anonymous

Nothing could be finer
Than to climb your Carolina,
  In the morning.

Then's the time that she is best,
When she's had a little rest,
  At dawning.

Then there's no one knocking
At the old front door,
Or rattling on the door-knob—
O Gawd, it used to make me sore.

You lie right beside her,
And climb right astride 'er,
  In the morning.

Her little buttercup starts
To cuddle up and pucker up,
  At dawning.

Night-time is the right time
Some people say;
But I will take the morning
Or I'll play a matinee—

For nothing could be sweeter
Than to have a little cheater,
  In the morning.

A SPORT MODEL TO A TRUCK

Anonymous

I seat myself to write you
  Just a wee short letter, Bess,
To inform you that my speeding
  Days are over now, I guess;
For I'm laid up in the junk-pile
  Wih others of my kind,
While sturdy-going trucks like you
  Have left me far behind.

Now, the reason that I'm laid-up
  In the shop for quite a spell,
Is a simply little story
  That, in rhyme, I'll try to tell.
I know you're sympathetic
  And will listen like a friend,
For the story's quite pathetic,
  With a real untimely end.

I was stepping out last evening,
  Making sixty miles an hour,
For my batteries were charged,
  And I had pep and power:
But there never was a pleasure
  That trouble couldn't spoil,
And I got a double measure
  When I started pumping oil.

So I went to see the doctor man—
  I mean to the garage—
And he said, "Your piston's leaking,
  And your battery's overcharged,
And your tappets need adjusting,
  And your sliding valve won't slip;
Your drain-cock's swelled to bursting,
  And your nuts have lost their grip."

"Your vacuum tank is out of juice,
  It won't work with a choke;
And your front nuts all are loose—
  Your springs are bent and broke,
Your steering gear is out of line,
  Your hot-spot's mighty cold,
The oil is running out behind—
  You've simply lost control."

SALLY: PARODY

Anonymous

I don't know what's become of Sally—
It was no fault of mine;
I wonder what's become of Sally—
I put her in the hay,
And then I went away.
Of course I must admit,
I rode her quite a bit,
But, from what I know now,
Someone else was doin' it.
I wonder what's become of Sally,
That old mare of mine.

OUT AT WAIKIKI

DON BLANDING

Out at Waikiki by the sobbing sea,
   In a district rather sporty,
In a banyan's shade lived a virgin maid
   Who was just this side of forty.

She did not go to a movie show,
   For she had no one to take her;
And she did not stray from the narrow way,
   Because nobody tried to make her.

But I wish to state that just this date
   She was Waikiki's one virgin,
Though some were sure that the girl was pure
   Because she'd had no urgin'.

But a dirty cat in a nearby flat,
   Whose morals were quite elastic,
Laid a low-lived plan to ruin Anne,
   With methods sly but drastic.

She stopped one day in a casual way
   To ask about Anne's persian,
Then said, "Oh, look at this lovely book,
   It's a new, uncensored version,

Of *Vermilion Sin* by Helliner Grynn,
   I'm sure you'll find it stirring."
With a knowing look she left the book,
   Despite Anne's chaste demurring.

In a wicker chair, all unaware
   Of her neighbor's wicked scheming,
Anne took a look through the borrowed book,
   And it set her wildly dreaming.

73

Each gilded sin that Helliner Grynn
　　Described with skill uncanny,
Stirred a strange unrest in the withered breast.
　　Of simple virgin Anne.

With a vision clear she saw how dear
　　Was the virtue that she'd been shielding,
And she longed for the charms of a lover's arms,
　　And the joys of weakly yielding.

In wild despair she tore her hair
　　Then cried to the stars above her:
"I'll end my state of a celibate,
　　I'll get me a hard-boiled lover."

With a frantic wail she cleared the rail
　　Of the porch with a leap gazellish,
And headed straight for her neighbor's gate
　　And the light in her eyes was hellish.

"I'll steal her rouge and her high-heel shoes—
　　The ones she wears on Mondays—
And I think I'll get her pink georgette
　　And silk embroidered 'undies'. "

Before her glass this aged lass
　　Sat down—it was really tragic—
And you would have cried as the virgin tried
　　To work a vampire's magic.

It was half-past ten when she left her den,
　　Feeling wild and very flighty,
As she boldly strode down Kalia Road
　　In her filmy chiffon nightie.
Underneath a tree at Waikiki
　　Was a sailor drinking madly,
It was rotten gin and it scorched his chin,
　　But he needed cheering badly.

For he was blue, and gin he knew,
    Would cheer his disposition.
Then he raised his eyes and to his surprise
    Saw a lovely apparition.

"My gob, my gob," he heard her sob,
    "My hero, my adorer."
It was Annie there, and her frenzied stare
    Quite startled the man before her.

He jumped to his feet for a quick retreat,
    But Anne, with a gesture quicker
Than a bullet's hum, seized the bottle of rum
    And drank the remaining liquor.

"Well, strike me pink," said the gob, "I think
    This jane is drunk or dippy.
But she looks all there, and I don't care
    If her figure is too hippy.

So he caught the maid as she dizzily swayed
    To his arms, and he quickly kissed her.
And he heard her moan like a saxaphone,
    As the first kiss raised a blister.

Oh, I can't write of that hectic night,
    My description would be pallid.
And anyway, the things I'd say
    Don't belong in a proper ballad.

But the papers state that next morning late
    On a beach by the broad Pacific,
They found Anne dead. But the papers said
    That her smile was beatific.

MADAME DU BARRY
DON BLANDING

Madame Du Barry
Was a lively old fairy
Who sold herself to a king;

She got jewels and riches
While other poor bitches
Stayed pure and got never a thing.

A LITTLE SONG
Anonymous

Listen to me and my little song,
And I'll tell you how a guy went wrong.
I used to live with aunty who was old and wealthy.
She had a servant girl who was fat and healthy.

I tried my best to get 'er to lay the leg,
Or take her in the woodshed on my peg:
No matter how I tried I didn't seem to figure,
So I think to this day, she was a gold-digger.

I sneaked 'round the back one night goin' to bed,
And caught her with her head in a barrel gettin' bread;
A chance like that, of course, I couldn't pass,
So, I histed up her skirts, and oosed it in her ass.

To think of worse luck; My God! I know I can't;
For, when she turned around, Great guns, it was my aunt!

76

SAM McCALL'S SONG

JIM TULLY

My name is Sam McCall
And I come from Donegal,
And I have no balls at all,
    Balls at all.

Oh, my name is Sam McCall—Sam McCall—
And I'm the greatest stud that ever had a stall,
    Had a stall.

Oh, I kicked the boards all out
When the women came about;
Now, I have no balls at all,
    Balls at all.

There can be no room for balls
When your penis fills the stalls,
    Fills the stalls.

Oh, the girlies laugh and sing
At the joy I always bring,
    Damn it all,
    Damn it all,
    Damn it all.

Oh, when I was just a lad,
My mother and my dad
Had put me in a tent to hide it all,
    Hide it all.

For they knew when girls discover
A big penis on a lover,
It would be the last of any lad from Donegal,
    Donegal.

And when Barnum came to Dublin,
He my father kept a-troublin'
To make a circus freak of Sam McGall,
    Sam McCall.

For he knew that all the women
With passion would be swimmin'
To get a private look at Sam McCall,
    Sam McCall.

THE YOUNGEST
Anonymous

She lay stark naked
Between the sheets,
So nice and fat and chubby;
And I myself beside her lay,
My hand upon her bubby.
I kissed her lips in crazy glee,
And 'neath her chin did chuck her:
Our thighs did intermingle,
And I began to fuck her.
"Pull out," she cried, "pull out! pull out,
Or I'll get me into trouble."
I did, and on her snow-white breast
That stream did squirt and bubble.
I looked into her frightened face
And, with a smile of mirth,
I said, "I guess that is the youngest child
That you have ever nursed."
She scooped it up with one fair hand,
And, with a glad ha ha,
She threw the load into my face
And said, "Child, go kiss your pa!"

YOUR RADIATORS BURSTED
Anonymous

Your radiator's bursted,
  And your dust-pan's on the bum;
Your gearshift's dry and rusted,
  And you cannot go or come.

Your four-wheel brakes have lost their grip
  As anyone can tell—
Your clutch is loose and bound to slip;
  Your rear-end's shot to hell.

Your sparkplugs fail to get the juice,
  Your lights are on the bum.
Your rear-wheel lugs are mighty loose,
  You've sure been going some.

Your windshield's broke, your starter's stuck,
  The rear-end lights won't burn;
In fact, old top, you're out of luck
  And hardly worth a durn.

I'll get the parts I know you need:
  Some monkey glands and such,
But you must cut down on your speed,
  And not go out so much;

For your rambling days, old top,
  Are over now, and past.
It's not because you ran the race,
  It's 'cause you ran too fast!

TEASE

D. H. LAWRENCE

I will give you all my keys,
   You shall be my chatelaine,
You shall enter as you please,
   As you please shall go again.

When I hear you jingling through
   All the chambers of my soul,
How I sit and laugh at you
   In your vain housekeeping role.

Jealous of the smallest cover,
   Angry at the simplest good;
Well, you anxious, inquisitive lover,
   Are you pleased with what's in store?

You have fingered all my treasures,
   Have you not, most curiously,
Handled all my tools and measures
   And masculine machinery?

Over every single beauty
   You have had your little rapture;
You have slain, as was your duty,
   Every sin-mouse you could capture.

Still you are not satisfied,
   Still you tremble faint reproach;
Challenge me I keep aside
   Secrets that you may not broach.

Maybe yes, and maybe no,
   Maybe there are secret places,
Altars barbarous below,
   Elsewhere halls of high disgraces.

Maybe yes, and maybe no,
    You may have it as you please,
Since I choose to keep you so,
    Suppliant on your curious knees.

IN MOBILE

Anonymous

Oh, the men they wash the dishes in Mobile,
Oh, the men they wash the dishes in Mobile,
    Oh, the men they wash the dishes
    And they dry them on their britches,
    Oh, the dirty sons-of-bitches in Mobile!

The cows they all are dead in Mobile,
The cows they all are dead in Mobile,
    The cows they all are dead
    So they milk the bulls instead,
    Because babies must be fed in Mobile!

Oh, they teach the babies tricks in Mobile,
Oh, they teach the babies tricks in Mobile,
    Oh, they teach the babiets tricks
    And by the time that they are six,
    They suck their fathers' pricks in Mobile!
Oh, the eagles they fly high, in Mobile,
Oh, the eagles they fly high, in Mobile,
    Oh, the eagles they fly high
    And from way up in the sky,
    They shit squarely in your eye, in Mobile!

81

IVY AND I AND GRANDFATHER'S CHAIR
Anonymous

The farmer was a deacon,
His wife was long of jaw
And their house was sad and lonely
As the first amoeba was.

The farmer worked me weary,
The woman starved me thin;
Alone their daugher loved me
And I loved her alone.

Yet

Satan came to tempt us
Behind grandfather's chair.
Still as a ghost was the empty house,
Warm in the summer night,
Echoing ancestors' footsteps,
Creaking at sudden winds—
The family was at revival
And she and I at home.
There was the open bible
For those who would to read,
A remarkable book,
But my fingers shook
In that cosy nook,
For the wisdom of the ancients
We must always learn anew.

I searched:

I know that my Redeemer liveth,
Praise ye the Lord, cry they;
He certainly rates some credit
For keeping them all away.

Tomorrow's chores are lighter;
Tomorrow's sun will set,
And hell will fire brighter
When the devil drags his net.

For

In it he will find
Her and me
Beside grandfather's chair
Once again.

She smiles and never tells
And the church will ring its bells
Every Sunday,
And the church will toll its knells
For the fools who fear its spells
Before they ever knew
Joy is life.

It's flames of hell that dance
And the lights of hell that shine
And the bells of hell that peal
For the blood of hell is wine!

Yes

Upon grandfather's chair
She was mine.

POOR OLD DICK
Anonymous

At the close of our existence,
  When we've climbed life's golden stairs
And the chilly winds of Autumn
  Rudely toss our silvery hairs;

When we feel our manhood ebbing,
  And we're up to life's last ditch,
And we find our faithful Peter
  Sleeping soundly at the switch;

God Almighty! ain't it awful!
  Don't it make you deathly sick,
When the painful fact confronts you
  That you've got a lifeless dick?

Ain't it sad for us to know
  That when we take him on the street,
That he ne'er again will wrestle

That he ne'er again will bristle
  With the pussies that we meet?
  On a wet and windy day,
When some maiden shows her stocking
  In that naughty, funny way?

Oh, my poor old loyal kingpin,
  How my heart goes out to you.
For I cannot but remember
  All the stunts you used to do.

How I charmed the maids and maidens,
  And the dashing widows too,
How you had the whole push wishing
  For just a little bit of you.

Don't you think that I've forgotten,
　When each dear girl you tried,
I could never make you quit her 'til
　She cried, "I'm satisfied."

Think you then that I'll forget you,
　Just because you are so dead,
And because when I command you,
　You cannot raise your head?

No indeed, my valiant comrade,
　Naught shall rob you of your fame!
Henceforth you'll be my pisser,
　And I'll love you just the same.

⌒

A TOAST

Anonymous

A social glass
And a social lass
Go very well together.
But a social lass
With a social ass
I think a damn sight better.
Here's to the glass,
And the lass, and the ass,
May we meet in all kinds of weather;
We'll drink from the glass,
And feel of the ass,
And make the lass feel better.

CHRISTOPHER COLUMBO

Anonymous

In fourteen hundred and ninety-two,
A dago from I-taly
Walked the streets of Sunny Spain
A-shouting, "Hot tamalie!"

> *He knew the world was round-O—*
> *His balls hung to the ground-O—*
> *That Dago-bastard-with-the-seven-year-itch,*
> *That syphillitic son-of-o-bitch*
> *Was Christopher Columbo.*

Columbo went unto the Queen
And asked for ships and cargo,
And said, "I'm a dirty son-of-a-bitch
If I don't bring back Chicago.

Chorus:

Columbo paced upon the deck,
He knew it was his duty
He laid his wang into his hand
And said, "ain't that a beauty."

Chorus:

A little girl walked up the deck
And peeked in through the keyhole,
He knocked her down upon her brown
And shoved it in her peehole.

Chorus:

She sprang aloft, her pants fell off,
The villain still pursued her;
The white of an egg ran down her leg,
The son-of-a-bitch had screwed her.

Chorus:

Each sailor on Columbo's ship
Had each his private knothole,
But Columbo was a superman
And he used a padded porthole.

Chorus:

Columbo had a cabin boy,
He loved him like a brother;
And every night they went to bed
And laid upon each other.

Chorus:

For forty days and forty nights
They sailed in search of booty;
They spied a whore upon the shore—
My God, she was a beauty.

Chorus:

All the men jumped overboard,
A-shedding coats and collars;—
In fifteen minutes, by the clock,
She made ten thousand dollars.

Chorus:

Those were the days of no clap cure;
The doctors were not many
The only doc' that he could find
Was a son-of-a-bitch named Benny.

Chorus:

Columbo strode up to the doc',
His smile serene and placid;—
The God-damned doc' burned off his cock
With hydrochloric acid.

Chorus:

WHEN I WAS YOUNG
Anonymous

When I was young and foolish
  I used to take delight
To go to balls and dances,
  And stay out late at night.

'Twas at a ball I met him,
  He asked me for a dance.
I knowed he was a sailor
  By the buttons on his pants.

His shoes were neatly polished,
  His hair was neatly combed,
And when the dance was over
  He asked to see me home.

As we walked home together
  I heard the people say,
"There goes another girlie
  That's being led astray."

'Twas on my father's doorstep
  That I was led astray,
'Twas in my mother's bedroom
  That I was forced to lay.

He laid me down so gently—
  He raised my dresses high;
He said, "Now, Maggie darling,
  Take it now, or die."

"Here is a half-a-dollar
  For the damage I have done,
For soon you will have children,
  A daughter or a son."

"If it is a daughter,
  Take her on you knee;
But if it's a son, then
  Send him out to sea."

"I hope, next time I see you,
  That you'll remember me,
And thank God for the blessing
  That I have brought to thee."

MARY'S LITTLE LAMB

Anonymous

Mary had a little lamb,
  Its fleece was white as snow;
And everywhere that Mary went
  The lamb was sure to go.

It followed her to the barn one day
  For eggs she was to hunt;
It stuck its nose beneath her clothes
  To get a whiff of cunt.

Now, Mary was a naughty girl
  And didn't give a damn;
She let him have another whiff
  And killed the god-damned lamb.

ABALONE SONG

GEORGE STERLING

In Carmel Bay the people say,
　　We feed the Lazaroni
On caramels and cockle-shells,
　　And hunks of abalone.

O some throw rice, and some throw dice
　　And some throw cascaroni,
But Eve, by hell, will throw a spell
　　Around the abalone.

O, some folks boast of quail on toast
　　Because they think it's tony,
But my tomcat gets nice and fat
　　On hunks of abalone.

He hides in caves beneath the waves,
　　His ancient patrimony;
Race suicide will ne'er betide
　　The fertile abalone.

I telegraphed my better half
　　By Morse, or by Marconi;
But when in need of greater speed
　　I send an abalone.

O, some think that the Lord is fat,
　　And some that he is bony;
But as for me I think that he
　　Is like an abalone.

THE JOLLY TINKER

Anonymous

There was a jolly tinker
   And he came from Dungaree;
With a half a yard of fungus
   Hanging down below his knee.

   Oh, his long, long dillywhacker,
   Over-grown kidney-cracker,
   Looking for a scrimmage
   Around the belly whang.

The landlady's daughter
   Coming from the ball,
Saw the jolly tinker
   Lashing piss against the wall.

   Oh, his long, long dillywhacker,
   Over-grown kidney-cracker,
   Looking for a scrimmage
   Around the belly whang.

O tinker! O tinker!
   I'm in love with you,
O tinker! O tinker!
   Will a half a dollar do?

   For your long, long dillywhacker,
   Over-grown kidney-cracker,
   Looking for a scrimmage
   Around the belly whang.

Oh, he screwed her in the parlor,
   He fucked her in the hall,
And the servant said, "By Jesus,
   He'll be cramming on us all."

With his long, long dillywhacker,
Over-grown kidney-cracker,
Looking for a scrimmage
Around the belly whang.

"O daughter! O daughter!
  You were a silly fool
To get busy with a man
  With a tool like a mule."

Oh, his long, long dillywhacker,
Over-grown kidney-cracker,
Looking for a scrimmage
Around the belly whang.

"O mother! O mother!
  I thought I was able,
But he split me up the belly,
  From the cunt up to the navel."

With his long, long dillywhacker,
Over-grown kidney-cracker,
Looking for a scrimmage
Around the belly whang.

——

CHANSON ANTIQUE

Anonymous

Gather ye rosebuds while ye may,
  Old time is still a-flying;
And the penis which is tiff today
  Tomorrow will be dying.

THE ENGINEER'S SONG

Anonymous

The runaway engine came down the track,
  And she blew, she blew;
The runaway engine came down the track,
  And she blew, she blew;
The runaway engine came down the track,
With her lever pushed up and her throttle pushed back,
  And she blew, blew, blew,
    The son-of-a-bitch, she blew.

The flagman he stood way out in the grass—
The staff of the flag ran up his ass.

Chorus:

The switchman he stood at the God-damned switch
And ditched the God-damned son-of-a-bitch.

Chorus:

The conductor he looked and he saw the wreck
And shit flew up the back of his neck.

Chorus:

The fireman he was shoveling coal—
The shovel handle ran up his asshole.

Chorus:

The engineer he stood at the throttle
Trying to piss in the neck of a bottle.

Chorus:

The porter stood at the stateroom door
Looking up the leg of a whore.

Chorus:

A big fat wench was riding the front
And a red-hot coal flew up her cunt.

Chorus:

JOCK McLAREN'S BIRDIE
Anonymous

Jock McLaren was a Hielan' mon:
He hailed from Brook Murray—
Be bought him a kilt o' the real McLaren
That na mair than covered his birdie.
The kilt with the weather began to shrink,
Till it scarcely reached his heardie.
Then Jock was shocked one day to find
That na mair it covered his birdie.
To buy a new ane cost mony baubers,
And Jock couldna wear his god one;
And to cut a piece off his birdie's head
Clearly was out of the question.
So he thot and he thot,
And he mair than thot,
'Til a thot thru his head came a-fartin'
He painted he tip of his birdie's head,
And ye na could tell it from the tartin.

THE NEW MAUD MULLER
Anonymous

Maud Muller on a Summer's day
Raked the meadows sweet with hay,
Beneath her torn hat glowed the wealth
Of simple beauty and rustic health.

She little dreamed that the man from town
Would get onto the charms beneath her gown—
The Judge rode slowly down the lane,
Stroking his horse's chestnut mane.

The Judge had been up the previous night
At a game of draw that was *out of sight*.
His friends filled him up with villainous budge,
And he left the game a busted Judge.

He did not despond or get a bit blue,
For the following week his salary was due;
But his nut was swelled and his tongue was thick,
And his brains were heated and so was his prick.

For a feverish jag, with its other arts,
Heats up the prick like other parts.
He dreamed of tail all along the lane,
But there was no tail, so he stroked the mane.

And he saw Maud Muller standing there
With her little tin cup and ankles bare,
And the idea struck him mighty quick—
"I'll quench my thirst, and please my prick."

"Please," said the Judge with a secret wink,
"I'm very dry, can I have a drink?"
She stooped where the cool spring bubbled up,
And filled for him the small tin cup.

95

With a start he saw in its mirrored glare
That she wore no pants, and her box was bare.
"Thanks," said the Judge, "a sweeter draught
From fairer hands was never quaffed."

He stood there waiting, still calling for more,
For so much true art he'd ne'er seen before.
Wiht fixt eyes he'd taken his thirty-third drink
When her box, true to nature, gave a definite wink.

Had it not been for this 'twould be safe to say
The Judge would be drinking to this very day.
The wink settled the business for his Honor that day,
He went off in his pants, and went on his way.

A WARNING

Anonymous

Come all you maids take warning,
Take a tip from me,
Never trust a sailor
An inch above your knee.

He'll swear that he will marry,
He'll promise to be true,
But when he's picked your cherry,
He'll say, "To hell with you."

WHY DOGS LEAVE A NICE FAT BONE

Anonymous

The dogs once held a meeting
  They came from near and far;
Some came in automobiles,
  Some came in a car.

But before, inside the hall,
  They were allowed to take a look,
They had to take their assholes off,
  And hang them on a hook.

They all walked in, one by one,
  Mother, son and sire,
But no sooner were they seated
  Than someone hollered, "Fire!"

Then they all rushed out in a bunch,
  They had no time to look;
So each one grabbed an asshole
  And ran it off the hook.

They got their assholes all mixed up,
  It made them awfully sore.
To think they'd lost the asshole
  They'd always worn before.

And that's the reason why
  When you go down the street,
A dog will stop and swap a smell
  With every dog he meets.

And that's the reason why
  A dog will leave nice fat bone,
To smell another's asshole,
  In hopes to find his own.

DRUNK LAST NIGHT

Anonymous

Drunk last night,
Drunk the night before,
Going to get drunk tonight
If I never get drunk no more.
I am as happy as can be
For I am a member of the souse familie.

Glorious! Glorious!
One keg of beer for the four of us,
Glory be to God there are no more of us,
For the four of us can drink it all alone.

BERRIES

Anonymous

Berries, berries, all kinds of berries,
Chancres on her ass like California cherries,
   The first time I hit her
   I nearly broke her shitter,
Down where the Hasiampa flows.

A PERSIAN KITTY
Anonymous

A persian kitty, perfumed and fair,
Strayed out through the kitchen door for air,
When a tomcat, lean, and lithe, and strong,
And dirty and yellow, came along.

He sniffed at the perfumed persian cat,
As she strutted about with much eclat,
And, thinking a bit of time to pass,
He whispered, "Kiddo, you sure got class."

"That's fitting and proper," was her reply
As she arched the whiskers over her eye.
"I'm ribboned; I sleep on a pillow of silk,
And daily they bathe me in certified milk."

"Yet we're never contented with what we've got,
I try to be happy, but happy I'm not;
And I should be joyful, I should indeed,
For I certainly am highly pedigreed."

"Cheer up," said the tomcat with a smile,
"And trust your new-found friend a while.
You need to escape from your backyard fence.
My dear, all you need is experience."

New joys of life he then unfurled,
As he told her tales of the outside world;
Suggesting at last with a luring laugh
A trip for the two down the Primrose Path.

The morning after the night before,
The cat came back at half past four
The innocent look in her eyes had went,
But the smile on her face was the smile of content.

And in after-days when children came,
To the persian kitty of pedigreed fame,
They were not persian, but black and tan,
And she told them their pa was a traveling man.

—

A LETTER FROM THE POSTMASTER

Anonymous

Sir: I'm sending you a token
Of a buggy whip that's broken
    And of footprints on the dash-board upside down.
There are grease-spots on the cushion
And there's evidence of pushin'
    And our daughter Venus hasn't come aroun'.

The Answer:

I'm the guy that done the pushin'
Put the grease-spots on the cushion,
    Made the foot-prints on the dashboard upside down;
But since I had your daughter Venus,
I've had trouble with my penis,
    And I wish I'd never seen your God-damned town!

CHAMBERLYE
Anonymous

Von Hindenberg, Von Hindenberg,
  You are a funny creature;
You've given the cruel war
  A new and funny feature.

You'd have us think while every man
  Is bound to be a fighter,
The women, bless their hearts,
  Should save their pee for nitre.

Von Hindenberg, Von Hindenberg,
  Where did you get the notion
Of sending barrels 'round the town
  To gather up the lotion?

We thought a woman's duty
  Was keeping house and diddling,
But now you've put the dears
  To patriotic piddling.

Von Hindenberg, Von Hindenberg,
  Pray do invent a neater
And somewhat less immodest way
  Of making your saltpetre.

For fraulien fair of golden hair,
  With whom we all are smitten,
Must join the line and jerk her brine
  To kill the bloomin' Briton.

Von Hindenberg, Von Hindenberg,
  We read in song and story
How many tears in all the years,
  Have sprinkled fields of glory;

But ne'er before have women helped
　　Their braves in bloody slaughter,
'Til German beauties dried their tears
　　And went to making water.

No wonder Von, your boys are brave!
　　Who would not be a fighter,
If every time he shot his gun
　　He used his sweetheart's nitre.

And, vice versa, what would make
　　An Allied soldier sadder,
Than dodging bullets fired from
　　A pretty woman's bladder?

We've heard it said a subtle smell
　　Still lingers in the powder,
The battle-smoke grows thicker still,
　　And the din of battle louder;

That there is found to this compound—
　　A serious objection—
A soldier cannot take a sniff
　　Without having an erection.

And it is clear now why desertion
　　Is so common in your ranks;
An Arctic nature's badly needed
　　To stand Dame Nature's pranks.

A German cannot stand the strain.
　　When once he's had a smell,
He's got to have a piece or bust—
　　The Fatherland to hell.

MY LULU

Anonymous

I wish I was a diamond
  Upon my Lulu's hand,
And every time she wiped her ass
  I'd see the promised land.

Bang away my Lulu,
Bang away good and strong;
Oh, what'll we do
For a damn good screw
When our Lulu's dead and gone?

I wish I was the pee-pot
  Beneath my Lulu's bed,
For every time she took a piss
  I'd see her maidenhead.

Chorus:

My Lulu had a baby,
  She named it Sunny Jim,
She dropped it in the pee-pot
  To see if he could swin.

Chorus:

First it went to the bottom,
  And then it came to the top,
When my Lulu got excited
  And grabbed it by the cock.

Chorus:

I wish I was the candle
  Within my Lulu's room,
And every night at nine o'clock
  I'd penetrate her womb.

Chorus:

My Lulu's tall and sprightly,
　　My Lulu's tall and thin,
I caught her by the railroad track
　　Jacking off with a coupling-pin.

Chorus:

I took her to the Poodle Dog,
　　Up on the seventh floor,
And there I gave her seventeen raps
　　And still she called for more.

Chorus:

My Lulu was arrested;
　　Ten dollars was the fine—
She said to the Judge,
　　"Take it out of this ass of mine."

Chorus:

———

L'ONGLE DE SYRINX

IBYKOS DE RHODES

The most admirable qualities in the world,
You possess
O Syrinx!
I am your acknowledged slave—
But, on the next occasion,
Pare more carefully
The nail of your virile finger:
You have scratched me!

104

LITTLE BUT NICE

Anonymous

A little kiss, a little smile,
A handclasp every little while;
A little whisper in the ear
That no one else may ever hear;
A little pressure of the foot
Upon your snugly buttoned boot,
A scribbled note, a little date
To meet you when the hour is late.
A little room in some hotel
A little promise not to tell;
A little drink when we are through.
A little fussing in a chair,
A little mussing of the hair
A little bathroom all in white,
A little turning down the light;
A little shirtwaist laid aside,
A little bust that tries to hide
A little skirt laid on a chair,
A little suit of underwear
That comes off with a little teasing,
And shows a little form most pleasing;
A little blush, a little sigh,
A little promise, bye and bye;
A little bed of shining brass,
A little turning off the gas;
A little nightrobe mostly lace,
More kisses, and a tight embrace.
A little wrestling in the gloom,
A deep sigh, and a quiet,
A little pair of hearts that beat,
A little effort to repeat ;
A little towel, maybe two,
A little snuggling up to you,

A little sleep 'til half past four
A little teasing for some more;
A little fussing while we dress,
A cigarette and a caress,
A little bill, a little tip,
A little parting at the lip;
A little stealing down the stair,
A little secret we can share;
A little weariness next day
As little children after play;
A little wish that you and I
May have another bye and bye.

LE CADI PERCLUS

HAROLD GREENTHAL

O venerable Cadi,
Nothing now remains
Of your voluptuous vigor
Of yesterday.

Your poor heart is cold,
Your body is crippled,
Your face is seamed with wrinkles
And love has strung bulging pouches
Under your eyes.

Your sex, which hangs pendant
At the base of your belly,
Is like a soft banana of Ispahan
Between two shrivelled oranges
From Damas.

SNAPOO
Anonymous

Oh madam, oh madam, your daughter's too fine—
  Snapoo!
Oh madam, oh madam, your daughter's too fine
To sleep with a soldier from over the Rhine—

Tap o tap pater and van de go tater,
And shaker snap peter snapoo!

Oh mother, oh mother, I'm not too fine—
  Snapoo!
Oh mother, oh mother, I'm not too fine
To sleep with a soldier from over the Rhine—

Chorus:

Oh mother, oh mother, he's teasing me—
  Snapoo!
Oh mother, oh mother, he's teasing me,
He's tickling the hole I use to pee—

Chorus:

Oh mother, oh mother, he's on me yet—
  Snapoo!
Oh mother, oh mother, he's on me yet,
And if he don't stop I will certainly shit—

Chorus:

Eight months rolled by and the ninth did pass—
  Snapoo!
Eight months rolled by and the ninth did pass,
And a little dutch soldier marched out of her ass—

Chorus:

The little dutch soldier grew and grew—
    Snapoo!
The little dutch soldier grew and grew
And now he's chasing the chippies too —

Chorus:

—

*B A T T L E H Y M N O F T H E 58 T H

Anonymous

Eyes right! Assholes tight!
Foreskins to the front!
We're the boys that make the noise
And we're always after cunt .
We're the heroes of the night,
And we'd sooner fuck than fight,
We're the heroes of the foreskin fusileers!

* At the time of the signing of the Armistice the 58th had been
in the trenches without relief for ten weeks. Ordered back to
their base at Laon they entered the town out of control of their
* Field said his wift took the boy away on a visit,

BALLOCHY BILL THE SAILOR

Anonymous

"Who is knocking at my door,"
  Said the fair young maiden.
"Who is knocking at my door,"
  Said the fair young maiden.

"Open the door and let me in,"
  Said Ballochy Bill the sailor;
"Open the door and let me in,"
  Said Ballochy Bill the sailor.

"You may sleep upon the floor,"
  Said the fair young maiden.
"To hell with the floor, I can't fuck that,"
  Said Ballochy Bill the sailor.

"You may lie down at my side,"
  Said the fair young maiden.
"To hell with your side, I can't fuck that,"
  Said Ballochy Bill the sailor.

"You may lie between my thighs,"
  Said the fair young maiden.
"What've you got between your thighs?"
  Said Ballochy Bill the sailor.

"O, I've got a nice pin-cushion,"
  Said the fair young maiden.
"And I've got a pin that will just fit in,"
  Said Ballochy Bill the sailor.

"But what if we have a baby?"
  Said the fair young maiden.
"Strangle the bastard and throw him away,"
  Said Ballochy Bill the sailor.

"But what about the law, sir,"
  Said the fair young maiden.
"Kick the bleeders out on their ass,"
  Said Ballochy Bill the sailor.

"But what if there's an inquest?"
  Said the fair young maiden.
"Then shove the inquest up your cunt,"
  Said Ballochy Bill the sailor.

"And what about my paw and maw?"
  Said the fair young maiden.
"Fuck your maw, and bugger your paw,"
  Said Ballochy Bill the sailor.

"Whenever shall I see you?"
  Said the fair young maiden.
"Whenever shall I see you?"
  Said the fair young maiden.

"Never no more you dirty whore,"
  Said Ballochy Bill the sailor.
"Never no more you dirty whore,"
  Said Ballochy Bill the sailor.

———

KISSING

Anonymous

A man may kiss his wife goodby,
The rose may kiss the butterfly,
The wine may kiss the frosted glass,
And you, my friends, may kiss my ass.

HINKY DINKY PARLEY VOUS
Anonymous

The French they are a peculiar race,
    Parley vous!
The French they are a peculiar race,
    Parley vous!
The French they are a peculiar race.
They piss with their feet and fuck with their face,
    Hinky dinky,
    Parley vous!

Oh madam, oh madam, have you a fine wine,
    Parley vous!
Oh madam, oh madam, have you a fine wine,
    Parley vous!
Oh madam, oh madam, have you a fine wine
Fit for a doughboy from the line?
    Hinky dinky,
    Parley vous!

And pray, have you a daughter fine,
    Parley vous!
And pray, have you a daughter fine,
    Parley vous!
And pray have you a daughter fine
Fit for a doughboy from the line?
    Parley vous!
    Hinky dinky,

So up stairs and into bed,
    Parley vous!
So up stairs and into bed,
    Parley vous!
So up stairs and into bed;
The French girl lost her maidenhead—
    Hinky dinky,
    Parley vous!

The first three months she took it well,
  Parley vous!
The first three months she took it well,
  Parley vous!
The first three months she took it well
And then she began to swell like hell—
  Hinky dinky,
  Parley vous!

The second three months kept up the swell,
  Parley vous!
The second three months kept up the swell,
  Parley vous!
The second three months kept up the swell,
And then she began to grunt like hell—
  Hinky dinky,
  Parley vous!

The third three months kept up the grunt,
  Parley vous!
The third three months kept up the grunt,
  Parley vous!
The third three months kept up the grunt,
And a little marine jumped out of her cunt—
  Hinky dinky,
  Parley vous!

THE BUGLE CALL

Anonymous

Asshole, asshole, a soldier I would be,
And piss, and piss, and pistols on my knee;
Fuck you, fuck you, for curiosity,
To fight for cunt, for cunt, for counterie.

NO MORE A-ROVIN

Anonymous

And then I touched her on the knee,
    Mark well what I do say;
And then I touched her on the knee.
Says she, "young man you're rather free."

A-rovin, a-rovin, since rovin's been my ru-eye-in,
I'll go no more a-rovin' with you fair maid!

And then I touched her on the thigh,
    Mark well what I do say;
And then I touched her on the thigh.
Says she, "Young man you're rather high."

Chorus:

And then I touched her on the thatch,
    Mark well what I do say;
And then I touched her on the thatch.
Says she, "Young man that's my main hatch."

Chorus:

And then I slipped it to the blocks,
    Mark well what I do say;
And then I slipped it to the blocks.
Says she, "Young man I've got the pox."

Chorus:

WOULD YOU
Anonymous

If in this world there were but two,
And all the world were good and true,
And if you knew that no one else knew,
　　Would you?

If you had dreamed of pajamas blue
And a strange arm encircling you,
And then awoke and found it true,
　　Would you?

If all the world were good and bright,
And if I stayed with you all night,
Then if I turned out every light,
　　Would you?

If I were in a certain place
And we were sleeping face to face,
With naught between us but some lace,
　　Would you say good night?

HERE'S TO THE GIRL
Anonymous

Here's to the girl with pretty blue eyes,
Who wears red hose and has big thighs,
She has no cock, but that's no sin,
She has a nice little hole to put one in.

114

THAIS

NEWMAN LEVY

One time in Alexandria,
  The wicked city by the Nile,
Where night-life was a mania,
  And souls were only pawns the while,
There lived, historians report,
  A dame adventurous and game,
The pride of Nile's far-famed resort,
  And Thais was her name.

Nearby, in peace and piety,
  There dwelt a band of holy men
Avoiding all society,
  Who'd built a retreat for only men.
And in the desert's solitude
  They spurned all worldly pleasure,
And gave their lives to rectitude,
  To fasting, and to holy labor.

One monk who'd left the ranks of Baal.
  To join this group of holy men,
Was known to men as Athanael.
  His fame had spread to all the world.
At fasting or at prayer bouts
  No other could compare with him.
At grand and lofty prayer shouts
  He'd do the course with pep and vim

One night while sleeping heavily
  (From fighting with the devil
He'd gone to bed unsteadily
  While the burning sun was shining still)
He had a vision Freudian;
  And tho he was annoyed and ill,
He analysed, like Adrian,
  In the styles of Doctors Jung and Brill.

115

He dreamed of Alexandria,
　　The wicked city by the Nile;
A crowd of men were leering,
　　In a manner somewhat vile,
At Thais who was dancing there.
　　And Athanael, who thot them rude,
Observed her do the shimmy
　　In what artists call the nude.

Said he, "This dream fantastical
　　Disturbs my holy thots so well
Desires unmonastical
　　Assail I fear my monkish cell.
I've blushed up to my galleria
　　Viewing this girl's anatomy;
I'll go to Alexandria
　　And save her soul from Hell."

So pausing not to wonder where
　　He'd put his summer underclothes,
He quickly packed his evening wear,
　　His toothbrush and his silken hose,
To guard against the weather's bite;
　　He added a woolen sweater vest,
And bidding all the boys good night,
　　He started on his human quest.

The monk, tho warned and fortified,
　　On his arrival one sunny day
Was deeply shocked and mortified
　　To find debauchery in sway;
While some lay in a stupor sent
　　By booze prescribed by Doctor Gray,
The others all were acting
　　In a most immoral way.

116

Said he to Thais, "Pardon me,
   I got to put you wise to Hell,
And, tho this job is hard on me,
   That's what I came down here to tell.
What's all this sousin' gettin you?
   Let's hit the trail and all will be well.
Cut out this pie-eyed retinue
   And save yourself from Hell."

Spite of this bold astonishment
   She coyly answered, "So,"
Trying to hide astonishment,
   "You said a heaping mouthful, Bo.
This burg's a frost, I'm tellin' you.
   The brand of hooch you get for dough
Ain't like the stuff we used to brew,
   So let's pack up and go."

So forth from Alexandria,
   The wicked city by the Nile,
Across the desert sands they go
   And leave behind the city vile;
'Til Thais, parched and sweltering
   Beneath the blazing of the sun,
Takes refuge in a convent
   And the habit of a nun.

But now the monk is terrified
   To find his fears attack amain
His vows of holy chastity
   Which crack beneath the strain.
Like one who's toted home a jag,
   He cries out in his grief and pain,
"I'll sell my soul to see her do
   The shimmy once again.

117

Alas! His pleading amorous
   And passionate have come too late.
The courtesan filled with piety
   And prayer, has made her final date.
The monk says, "That's a joke on me,
   For that there dame to pass away;
I hadn't oughter passed her up
   The time I had it all my way."

THERE WAS AN OLD MAN

Anonymous

There was an old man sitting on a rock,
Watching little boys playing with their—
Agates and marbles in Springtime of yore;
While over in the bushes they watched a fat—
Brunette young lady sitting in the grass;
When she rolled over you could see her shapely—
Shoes and stockings that fit like a duck;
She said she was learning a new way to—
Bring up her children and teach them to knit;
As over in the bushes they were taking a—
Little companion down to the docks;
And said they would show him the length of their—
You may think this is bull-shit,
But it isn't, by God!

A MIRACLE

Anonymous

A hermit once lived in a beautiful dell,
And it is no legion, this that I tell,
So my father declared, who knew him quite well,
  The hermit.

He lived in a cave by the side of the lake,
Decoctions of herbs for his health he would take,
And only of fish could this good man partake,
  On Friday.
And most of his time he spent in repose,
Once a year he would bathe, both his body and clothes,
How the lake ever stood it, the Lord only knows,
  And He won't tell.

One day as he rose, dripping and wet,
His horrified vision three pretty girls met;
In matters of gallantry he wasn't a vet,
  So he blushed.

He grabbed up his hat that lay on the beach,
And covered up all that its wide brim would reach,
Then he cried to the girls in a horrified screech,
  "Go away!"

But the girls only laughed at his pitiful plight,
And begged him to show them the wonderful sight,
But he clung to his hat with all of his might,
  To hide it.

But just at this moment a villainous gnat
Made the hermit forget just where he was at,
He struck at the insect, and let go the hat—
  Oh horrors!

Now I have come to the thread of my tale;
At first he turned red, then he grew pale,
Then he uttered a prayer for prayers never fail,
   So 'tis said.

Of the truth of this tale, there is no doubt at all;
The Lord heard his prayer and answered his call:
Tho' he let go the hat, the hat didn't fall.
   Miracle!

GOOSEY BILL

Anonymous

We buried our old friend Bill today,
   A companion of pipe and bowl,
We've been on so many a drunk together
   Damn his good old soul.
I always had Bill bested
   When it came to drinking booze,
But the man who could beat Bill fucking
   Never walked in a pair of shoes.
He was always there with a bone on,
   And ready to spill a lump;
Said he'd give his place in heaven
   For a first class piece of cunt.
It wasn't the booze that killed old Bill,
   Nor cunt that took his breath away,
But a fly crawled up his asshole
   And tickled poor old Bill to death.

WHANG

Anonymous

I'll tell you a little story,
   Just a story I have heard,
And you'll swear it's all a fable
   But it's gospel every word.

When the Lord made father Adam
   They say he laughed and sang,
And sewed him up the belly
   With a little piece of whang.

But when the Lord was finished
   He found he'd measured wrong;
For when the whang was knotted
   'Twas several inches long.

Said He, " 'tis but eight inches
   So I guess Ill let it hang."
So He left on Adam's belly
   That little piece of whang.

But when the Lord made mother Eve
   I imagine he did snort,
When he found the whang he sewed
   Her with was inches short.

" 'Twill leave an awful gap," said He,
   "But I should give a damn,
She can fight it out with Adam
   For that little piece of whang."

So ever since that day
   When Human life began,
There's been a constant struggle
   Twixt the woman and the man.

Women swear tney'll have the piece
    That from our belly hangs,
To fill the awful crack left when
    The Lord ran out of whang.

So let us not be jealous boys,
    With that which women lack,
But lend that little piece of whang
    To fill that awful crack.

THE RING OF HANS CARVER

J. T. SHIPLEY

What has she done that you should suspect her, Hans?
Is not your love enough to protect her, Hans?
Is she a fire stirred by so many fans
You must have power greater than any man's?

Hear then a wondrous thing:
    The weaver of this ring
    All other lovers bans,
Hans.

Hans woke, in his lusty pride,
To wreak his love on his bride,
What was the ring the dawn would bring?
He blushed, for his hand was pressed
In passion's nest. . . . .
And then Hans ruefully knew
His dream was true.

THE LOST GARTER
Anonymous

As I went down to Osbury town upon a market day,
By chance I spied a lady, a lady on her way;
She was going to market with her butter, eggs, and cream,
So we jogged along together, together on the green.

Jogging with this pretty maid, while jogging by her side,
By chance I sped her garter, her garter was untied;
For fear that she would lose it I resolved to tell her so—
Says I, "My dear young lady, your garter's hanging low."

"Oh since you've been so kind, since you've been so free,
Oh, since you've been so kind, won't you tie it up for me?"
"I will, yes I will, when we get to yonder hill."
And we jogged along together, together on the green.

On reaching the hill so pleasant was the scene,
On tying up her garter, such a sight was never seen.
She rolled up her lily-white robes and I rolled in between,
And we jogged along together, boys, together on the green.

Going on to market, her butter and eggs were sold—
But the losing of her maidenhead, it made her blood run cold;
"Oh, it's gone, let it go, he's the man that I adore—
For he's a fucking son-of-abitch and I'm a little whore."

THE BULL
Anonymous

Here's to the bull that roams the wood:
He does the cows and heifers good;
If it were not for his long, long rod,
We'd not have any beef, by God!

123

THE BACHELOR'S SON

Anonymous

Now, I am a bachelor, and I live by myself,
  And I work at the weaver's trade;
And the only thing that I ever did wrong,
  Was to ruin a fair young maid.

Oh, I wooed her in the summer time,
  And part of the winter time too;
But the only thing that I ever did wrong
  Was to keep her from the foggy foggy dew.

One night this maid came to my bedside,
  Where I lay fast asleep,
She laid her head upon my bed
  And there she began to weep.

She sighed, she cried, she darned near died,
  She said, "what shall I do?"
So I took her into bed, and I covered up her head,
  Just to keep her from the foggy foggy dew.

Now, I'm a bachelor and I live with my son,
  And I work at the weaver's trade;
And every time that I look into his face,
  He reminds me of that maid.

  Reminds me of the summer time,
  And part of the winter time too,
And the many many times that I took her in my arms,
  Just to keep her from the foggy foggy dew.

BALLAD OF SPEARMINT GUM

Anonymous

Says the boy to the girl, "Will you give me some?"
"I will," she said, "If you'll buy me some gum."

So the boy was nice and bought the gum,
And the girl agreed to give him some.

"Now this is a thing I've never done,
For a big stiff prick I always shun."

"But if it's half as nice as the gum I chew,
I know I'll like it as well as you."

So he laid her down upon the grass;
She chewed her gum, and wiggled her ass.

And the nearer she came to where she come,
The harder she chewed her spearmint gum.

All of a sudden, she grabbed him tight,
Gave a big grunt, squeezed with all her might;

Tears came to eyes as she swallowed her gum;
She almost passed out, and then she come.

~

A FOOL'S PRAYER

Anonymous

A fool there was and he made a prayer
To a rag, a bone, and a hank of hair;
He placed his bone in the hank o' hair,
But the fool was fooled, the rag was there.

I'M GETTING OLDER

Anonymous

I see my finish sure and surer,
    Every year;
For I am getting poor and poorer,
    Every year;
My wits are getting thicker,
With less capacity for liquor,
    Every year.

The women, they are sweeter,
    Every year;
There is more demand for Peter,
    Every year;
But mine, it gets no bigger,
And it's slower on the trigger,
And cuts less and lesser figure,
    Every year.

HIS GREATEST FEAR

Anonymous

Some folks die of whisky, and some folks die of beer,
And some folks di-a-betis, and some of di-a-rrhea;
But of all the dread diseases the one that I most fear,
Is the drip-drip-drip, and the drop-drop-drop
Of the red-headed gonorrhea.

HELL

E. A. VON KLEIM

Just what is meant by this word, *Hell?*
They sometimes say, *it's cold as hell.*
Sometimes they say, *it's hot as hell.*
When it rains hard, *it's hell,* they cry.
It's also, *hell,* when it is dry.
They *hate like hell* to see it snow.
It's a *hell of a wind* when it starts to blow.
Now, *how in hell* can anyone tell,
What in hell they mean by this word *hell?*
This married life is *hell* they say—
When he comes in late *there's hell to pay*—
When he starts to yell, *it's a hell of a note.*
It's *hell* when a kid you have to tote.
It's *hell* when the doctor sends his bills,
For *a hell of a lot* of trips and pills.
When you get this you will know real well
Just what is meant by this word *hell.*
Hell yes! Hell no! and *Oh hell!* too.
The hell you don't—the hell you do—
And *what in hell,* and *the hell it is—*
The hell with yours and *the hell with his—*
Now, *who in hell?* and *Oh hell, where?*—
And *what in hell do you think I care?*—
But *the hell of it is, it's sure as hell*
We don't know *what in hell is hell.*

THE SPANISH NOBILIO

Anonymous

There once was a Spanish Nobilio,
Who lived in an ancient castillio;
He was proud of his tra la la lillio,
And the works of his tweedle dum dee!

One day he went to the theatillio,
And there saw a lovely dancillio
Who excited his tra la la lillio,
And the works of his tweedle dum dee!

He took her up to his castillio
And laid her upon his sofillio,
Then inserted his tra la la lillio,
And the works of his tweedle dum dee!

Nine days later he saw the doctillio—
He had a fine dose of clapillio
All over his tra la la lillio,
And the works of his tweedle dum dee!

Now he sits in his castillio,
With a handful of cotton-wadillio;
He swabs off his tra la la lillio
And the works of his tweedle dum dee!

THE YOUNG MAN OF CALCUTTA

Anonymous

There was a young man of Calcutta
  Who practiced a curious trick:
He greased up his asshole with buttah
  And therein inserted his prick.

He adopted this measure so shady,
  Not for pleasure, nor power, nor pelf:
But merely because a young lady
  Had told him to go fuck himself.

FATE

Anonymous

With passion
Her lips were
Ashen.

With passion
His lips were
Ashen.

Ashes to ashes
Guts to guts.

AMOUR

Anonymous

Where, Ramadan gold moon to fasters,
There is a slight fair boy, my masters,
You may be sure to see draw near
A shiek, snow-bearded and severe,
Who has so studied lore of love
Below, behind, about, above,
With licit and with illicit,
That he could take degrees in it.
Between the lasses and the lads
He's lost his pleasant body pads,
A toothpick in a shroud is he,
But O, a moor for buggery!

They say his interest in woman
Is rather casual, if human;
But I can tell you, for a fact,
He holds his own in either act.
With bearded and with breasted youth
He seeks the principles of truth,
And in young concave, young convex,
Holds fair the balance of his sex. . . .
(With this proviso, certainly,
That he's a moor for buggery).

BANANAS

E. P. MATHER

Heavy bars of gold, or swaying,
  Or slow ripened in our presses,
Flasks of scent, with widows praying,
  Widows dreaming of caresses;

Buttered flesh like paste of cooking,
  Yellows of so bold a shape
Little girls cannot help looking,
  Hardly help surmise a rape.

———

LEMONS

E. P. MATHER

Snow that takes on saffrons,
  Silver turning gold
    Are lemons.

Moons which waver into suns,
  Chrysolite bells and manifold
    Are lemon, lemons.

Camphor ripening to corn light,
  Breasts that else could not be told
    Are lemons, lemons, lemons.

CHRISTMAS IN THE WORK'US

Anonymous

It was Christmas day in the work'us,
  The best day of the year;
And' the paupers h'all was 'appy
  For their guts was full o' beer.

The master of the work'us
  Strode through those dismal 'alls,
An' wished 'em Merry Christmas,
  An' the paupers h'answered, "Balls!"

This made the master h'angry,
  An' 'e swore by h'all the Gods,
They'd arve no Christmas puddin',
  The lousy lot of sods.

Up sprang a war-scarred vet'ran
  'Oo 'ad stormed the Khyber Pass,
"We don't want yer Christmas puddin',
  Shove it up yer fuckin' ass!"

~

PUNKT

JAMES JOYCE

Leftherhis
Secondbest
Leftherhis
Bestabed
Secabest
Leftabed!

132

THE BEAUTY LOVER

CLAIRE BU ZARD

The round, pink, laughing girl bathes,
And the thin, gray, silent girl watches.
. . . . . and afterwards,
When the bather dries herself,
And puts powder under her arms,
And lies down, like a sleepy flower,—
The gray girl catches her around the hips
Violently,
And kisses her:
Surprised, the pink girl draws away;
And the gray girl—
(Poor little lover of beauty)
Apologizes,
And is ashamed.

~

SLIM'S GAL

Anonymous

Slim's gal was tall and slender,
  My gal was short and low;
Slim's gal wore silks and satins,
  My poor gal wore calico.

Slim's gal was rich and sporty,
  My gal was poor and good.
Would I trade gals with Slim?
  You're God damned right I would!

SUSIE'S BEAU
Anonymous

Sister Susie got a beau;
Say, he ain't so gosh darned slow;
As a kisser he's right there,
Boy! he smacks her everywhere.
Just last Sunday I got hep—
Watched him kiss her on the step;
Came inside and sat in there,
And he kissed her on the chair;
Little later just for sport,
Kissed her on the davenport;
When he smacked her on the couch—
Sis just squeeled and hollered, "Ouch!"
When at night they stroll and talk,
He will kiss her on the walk;
And, you wouldn't think it true,
Kiss her on the Avenue!
In the street car, O he's neat—
Once he kissed her on the seat—
Talk about your pigs in clover,
He just kisses her all over.

~

BROWN EYES
Anonymous

Here's to the girl with eyes of brown,
Who makes her living upside down;
Fifteen cents is the regular price—
Give her a quarter, she'll do it twice.

THE DARING FLY
Anonymous

The little fly flew by the door,
Then flew into the grocery store:
He shit on the cheese, and shit on the ham,
Then he wiped his feet on the grocery man.

When the grocery man saw what he had done,
He went and loaded his gattling-gun;
Then he chased that fly all over the place,
And tried to shoot him square in the face.

But the little fly was awfully slick:
He showed the grocery man a trick.
He flew all around the store, and then
Went over and shit on the ham again.

And when he had finished his dirty work,
He went over and lit on the lady clerk;
And he climbed up her leg way past her knee,
And tickled her so she laughed with glee.

He fluttered so fast he made her sigh,
And she softly murmured, "Oh my, Oh my!"
Then she closed her legs and held her breath,
And poor little fly was smothered to death.

THE SPLIT
Anonymous

Here's to the split that never heals,
The longer you rub it the better it feels;
And all the soap this side of hell
Can't wash away that fishy smell.

135

THE MEPHIPHA ALPHABET

Anonymous

A is for Amour, that starts the affair;
B is for Bedroom, to which they repair
C is for Cigarettes, smokes in between;
D is for Drinks, that are frequently seen;
E is for Elevator, takes the pair up;
F is French Restaurant, such as the *Pup;*
G is for Girl, a regular jewel;
H is for Husband, the silly old fool;
I is for Illicit Love, long may it reign;
J is for Joy of it, bringing sweet pain;
K is for Kisses, you want more and more;
L is for Lingerie, strewn on the floor;
M is for Mephipha, God bless it, it's grand;
N for both Nature and Nudity stand;
O is for Oh, in the stillness of night;
P is for Passion, that makes all things right;
Q is for Quality, Quantity too;
R is for Resistance, found in but few;
S is for Skin of her, fair as a pearl;
T is for Technique, that would make your hair curl;
U is for Unity, greatest of joys;
V is for Virtue, that only annoys;
W for Whirling-spray, great old invention;
X for Expenses, needless to mention;
Y is for You, dear, inspiring this rhyme;
Z is for Zest of it, making all things sublime.

BOYHOOD
Anonymous

I know not how, what courage made me dare,
But, pillowed close, upon her bosom fair,
A truant hand went wandering far astray
And found—that night hath greater charms than day.
A mighty Mars, full statured in an hour,
From Great Athena's helmet, in his power
Sprang forth full armored at the will of Jove,
So sprang I forth equipped and armed for love.
With new-found strength, I ceased to be afraid
And something wild within me would not be stayed.
Disarmed, perhaps, by hungry widowhood,
She could not check me even if she would,
And kisses wild were riotously pressed
On starving lips too long left uncaressed,
And roses red upon the white flesh burned,
The while she murmured, "Child, where have you learned?"

THE CIVIL WHORE
Anonymous

The Postman came
   On the first of May,

The Policeman came
   The very next day,

Nine months later
   There was hell to pay;

Who fired the shot?
   The Blue or the Gray?

THE BEE AND THE COW
Anonymous

'Twas a sunny morn in June,
The bee had put his pipes atune,
And buzzed his way across the field.
And, while the birds their love songs spieled,
He buzzed and ate full many an hour,
Then crawled into a dainty flower
And curled himself up for a nap
The same as any drowsy chap.
A cow came browsing through the moor,
And towards the little fllowerlet bore.
Not knowing that the bee was there
She put it on her bill-of-fare.
So rudely wakened from his doze
His beeship's fiery temper rose—
"Old cow," he said, "I'll sting you deep
When I have finished with my sleep."
So, cuddled in his darksome den,
Eftsoon, he went to sleep again.
He slumbered on 'til early dawn,
But, when he awoke, the cow was gone!

PRIVATE PROPERTY
Anonymous

If I had a girl and she was mine,
I'd paint her tits with iodine,
And on her belly I'd paint a sign,
"Keep off the grass, this ass is mine."

DOWN IN NEW ORLEANS
Anonymous

When I was a servant girl way down in New Orleans,
My master was a king and my mistress was a queen;
And there I met a sailor from far across the sea,
And he's the son-of-a-bitch who started all my misery.
He asked me for a candle to light his way to bed,
He asked me for a handkerchief to tie around his head;
For I was young and pure and thought it was no harm
And I jumped into his bed to keep the sailor warm.
Next morning very early when I at last awoke
The sailor blithely handed me a dollar note.
Now all fair maidens please do take a tip from me:
Never let a sailor go an inch above your knee;
For I tried once and once is more than enough for me
The bastard left me with a dose of gonorrhea.

SARA JANE
Anonymous

There's a place not far from here
Where they sell anhauser beer.
There's a girl there is a darling
And I've got her on the string;
She's a peach, she's a dandy,
Tho she's knockkneed and she's bandy.

She carries her left wing in a sling,
She's got a shape just like a cook,
She's the terror of New York,
My cockeyed, consumptive Sara Jane.

THE NIGHT OF THE KING'S CASTRATION
Anonymous

'Twas the night of the king's castration,
   All the counts and the no-counts were there;
When the ladies went a-rear for libation
   And there tossed they huge gobs of manure.

Then there came to the court one hight Daniel:
   "You're a son-of-a-bitch," said the king,
"You're a son-of-a-bitch," said Daniel—
   Calling kings sons-of-sluts was common then.

But the king was mightily wrought,
   And his snot flung into the soup.
Then ordering his minions brought,
   He had Daniel cast unto the lions.

Any man would have died of fright
   But not Daniel, who boldly strode forth,
Grabbed a lion's left nut very tight,
   And mightily squeezed all his worth.

Then the lion cried, "Ouch, it tickles."
   "May I ask you what tickles," said Daniel.
Said the lion," My dear boy, testicles,"
   And he laughed 'til he was dead.

On the next day the court assembled
   In the great ampitheatre,
And the king and his court had gambled
   Many rupees of the realm.

Then the king missed his fair queen,
  And he called for the Lord Chancellor.
"Pray where is the queen, thou old bean?
  She should be at our party today."

Then the Lord High Chancellor responded,
  "She beshiteth herself in the crapper."
"Is there plenty of bungwad suspended
  On the royal nail for her ass?"

"She hath four and twenty ream
  Of the finest tissue made."
"'Tis well Sir, let none e'er dream
  Royal ass ever touched a corncob."

And the king went to the locker
  Where his private crapper stood,
And he shit three pounds of butter—
  And earned the name of King Dairyass.

At the end of his mighty crapping,
  On his way to his dignified court,
He looked down where the lions were scrapping
  And espied our Daniel alive.

"How's tricks in the hole?" said the king.
  "What hole," says Daniel. "Asshole," says the king.
"Suck it," says Daniel. And the judge
  Declared the drinks were on the king.

Once more the king asked for the queen
  And a smart young prick spoke up,
"She lies with the jester, sire," he said,
  "And the biggest liar's a slut!"

The queen came sweeping down the hall—
  "Greetings, Lord of the Sod," she said
"What sod do you mean?" cried out the king.
  "Lord of the sodomy," she said.

"And as for you," she added then,
  "You're not so much to me, you see,
For I could be king if I had to,"—
  "Two what?" he cried! "Balls," answered she.

So then they had a foreskin race,
  Where length and trigger-speed both counted.
"Daniel! Come forth!" said the king with his face—
  And Daniel came came fifth and lost the race!

~

WHEN I DIE

Anonymous

Oh, when I die, don't bury me at all;
Just pickle my balls in alcohol;
Put a bottle of booze at my feet and head
And if I don't drink it up, drink it up, drink it up,
You'll—know—I'm—dead!

OVER THE GARDEN WALL
Anonymous

I went out to pee behind a tree
  Over the garden wall,
And what I saw just filled me with glee,
  Over the garden wall.

At first it was dark, but at last I made out
A male and a female were there beyond doubt;
And I was not long guessing what they were about
  Under the garden wall.

The gent by the wall was young and tall,
The maid was fair beyond compare,
Her dress was up, and her ass was bare,
And little they dreamed that I was there
  Over the garden wall.

I saw a pair of delightful thighs
  Over the garden wall,
And a tool of most enormous size
  Over the garden wall.

I heard her exclaim, "What a beauty, dear Jim,
Go easy, old boy, as you stick him in;
Be easy at first or you'll split my vein."
  Over the garden wall.

The sight gave me a peculiar shock
  Over the garden wall,
I found I was rubbing my sensitive cock
  Near the garden wall.

All gone was my inclination to pee
  Over the garden wall,
For the girl, as she left, would have to pass me
  Over the garden wall.

143

DOWN THE LEHIGH VALLEY

Anonymous

It was down the Lehigh Valley in early Sixty Three;
   We were panning sand in the Rio Grande,
My cross-eyed partner, Bill, and me,
   When Bill got stuck on a gal named Nell.
Well, she warn't so goldarned bad,
   But he brought her up to the house to live,
And I was a rooty lad.

While cross-eyed Bill was panning in the creek
   As it trickled through the trees near by,
Nell and I'd be at it a-tearing off a trick.
   Well, Spring rolled by in the old Lehigh
And Nell dropped twins, you see:
   One was a cross-eyed son-of-a-bitch
And the other looked just like me.

A DOG FOR SALE

Anonymous

A nice brown dog, as sound as a ring,
   Will be eight years old if he lives 'til Spring.
He will piss on your carpet—shit on your grass—
   Has three white feet, and a hole in his ass.
His head bulges out, and his ass caves in,
   But he's a damn fine dog for the shape he's in.

DRIVING RULES

Anonymous

If she has not been driven before
   See that her inlet valves are greased,
Feel her crank and feel her shaft. Be sure
   Her toggle-joint and tail-light are fit.

When she begins to warm pull up her hood,
   Then you turn her over several times
And work the piston rods slowly but good
   Against the het-up cylinder head.

Now, carefully start on the lowest speed
   But when you feel her vibration begin,
And you feel her clutch take hold with greed,
   Open her up and drive it all in.

If she starts to shoot in her muffler
   Watch her transmission or her carburetor'll flood
And thus in trouble get her governor;
   And when she begins to boil over the hood,

Put on your brakes—then throw out your clutch,
   And wash her radiator out with water.
Pull down her hood—be careful with your touch—
   And chances are you'll have no trouble with her.

If some stranger has been running her
   And has got her all het up and soiled,
Be careful not to touch her radiator,
   For you are more than liable to get burnt.

THE MORTAL
Anonymous

Once upon a midnight dreary
When of smoking I was weary,
And had drunk up all my whisky
Only wishing there was more;
Suddenly there came a rapping
As of some fair female tapping
Tapping at my chamber door.
'Tis some chippy that's a-wishin'
To my room to gain admission.
Well, I'll rise and let her enter,
Enter though she be a whore,
Only that, and nothing more.

So I opened wide the portal,
And there stood such a mortal
As in all my living moments,
I had never seen before.
She had lost her upper garments,
And of all seductive varmints,
She was sure the warmest baby
Mortal woman ever bore;
And each palpitating bubby
Was so round and firm and chubby,
That my spirits rose within me,
Just my spirits, nothing more.

'Twas the fourteenth of December;
But more clearly I remember
When I woke up in the morning
Of December twenty-four—
Sequel of ten days before.

All that's left of what passed between us
Is one poor infected penis;
Drooping, red and retrospective,
Penitent, and very sore;
And that penis still is dripping,
Every morning, every evening,
Dripping on the bathroom floor.
And I murmur vows forgotten
Every time I change the cotton.
No more tapping, no more rapping,
No, never, nevermore.

—

JOLLY OLD MEDI

JAMES JOYCE

First he tickled her,
Then he patted her,
Then he passed the female catheter,
For he was a medical
Jolly old medi.

YANKEE DOODLE

Anonymous

Father and I went down to camp,
  Along with Cap'n Goodwin,
And there we saw the whores and pimps
  As thick as hasty pudding'.

Yanke Doodle, keep it up,
  Yankee Doodle dandy,
Mind the action and the pep,
  And with the girls be handy!

And there we saw a thousand men
  As rich as Squire David;
The cocks they wasted every day
  Iwish they could be saved.

Chorus:

The cunts they use up every day
  Would make a whore-house rich;
They have so many that, I'll be bound,
  They use 'em when they're mind ter.

Chorus:

And there I see a private's gun
  Large as a bullock pintle,
So deuced large it was he'd run
  It into father's cattle.

Chorus:

And every time he shot is off,
    So strong the force it spent,
The cows they couldn't stand the shock,
    And went like hell, they went.

Chorus:

I went as nigh to them myself
    As one would dare to venture,
And father went as nigh agin,
    I thought his hard was on him.

Chorus:

Cousin Simon grew so nervous,
    I thought he'd masturbate it,
It worked me so I jacked it off
    Behind a fat old trumpet.

Chorus:

And Cap'n Davis had a gun,
    With a dose of clap on't.
And he kept rubbing medicaments
    Upon the ruddied top on't.

Chorus:

And there I see a hookshop jane
    As big as mother's servant,
And every time they stuck it in 'er
Her yells were most elatant.

Chorus:

And there they frigged away like fun
    And played their cock-a-diddles,
And some had pricks as red as blood
    All hung about their middles.

Chorus:

The troopers they would gallop up
    And fart right in our faces,
It scared me almost half to death
    To see such farty faces.

Chorus:

I see a little pussy there
    All haired against the weather;
They pumped between its scarlet lips
    A mighty big bananer.

Chorus:

And there was Cap'n Washington
    With gentle whores about him;
They say his cock's so 'tarnal proud
    He cannot ride without 'em.

Chorus:

All this so scared me I run off,
Nor stopped, as I remember,
Nor turned about 'til I got home,
    Locked up in mother's chamber.

Chorus:

OVER THERE

Anonymous

Oh, the peters they grow small, over there,
Oh, the peters they grow small, over there,
Oh, the peter they grow small,
Because they work 'em for a fall,
Andthen eats 'em, tops and all, over there.

Oh, the pussies they are small, over there,
Oh, the pussies they are small, over there,
Oh, the pussies they are small,
But they take 'em short and tall,
And then burns their pricks and all, over **there.**

Oh, I wish I was a pimp, over there,
Oh, I wish I was a pimp, over there,
Oh, I wish I was a pimp,
For I'd give the boys a crimp,
With all my whorey blimps, over there.

Oh, they had a squirt for clap, over there,
Oh, they had a squirt for clap, over there,
Oh, they had a squirt for clap,
It was a potent clap trap,
And it burnt our pecker's cap, over there.

RECOLLECTIONS, A. E. F.
Anonymous

When this cruel war is over
    And we've laid aside our hates,
When we've crossed the bounding billow
    To our loved United States,
When I sleep in thin pyjamas,
    Not in sweater, socks and pants,
I will think about this billet
    Where I froze in Sunny France.

I'll go into my toilet room
    And find it always neat,
Warm and odorless and cleanly,
    With a polished oaken seat,
Where the pipes are never frozen,
    Then the budding poet grants
He will shiver when he thinks
    About the icy cans in France.

I'll slip into my bed at night
    Beneath a quilted spread,
That tucks in at the bottom
    While it reaches to my head.
Whether woman helps to warm it,
    Or I sleep alone, perchance,
I'll never miss the liver pad
    I froze beneath in France.

Each morning when I'm shaving,
    And the running water steams,
I'll think of freezing shaves abroad
    As odd fantastic dreams.
But when I see a chamber pot,
    There isn't any chance,
I'll forget the mug of amber ice
    Beneath my bed in France.

THE HAMBURG SHOW

Anonymous

Ladies and gents, are you ready? Larry turn the crank—

> *For we're going to the Hamburg Show,*
> *See the monkey and the wild kangaroo,*
> *And we'll all stick together in all sorts of weather*
> *For we're gonna see the whole show through.*

And in the next cage, we have the South American
Llama who roams the wild mountain ranges
Of the Andes, leaping from precipice
To precipice, and back to piss again.

> *Larry turn the crank, etc.*

And in the next cage, we have the Javanese Baboon
Who is so fat that every time time he winks his eye
He skins his prick. The ladies delight in throwing
Sand in his eyes to watch him masturbate.

Chorus:

And in the next cage we have the Australian Ostrich
Who, when frightened, sticks his head
Deep down into the desert sand and farts—
Hence the antipodal trade winds.

Chorus:

And in the next cage, we have the spotted leopard
Who has a spot for each day of the year.
You ask, lady, what he does in leap year?
Under his tail, madam, you will find the extra spot.

Chorus:

And in the next cage, we have the hippotamus
Who has a square ass-hole and eats mud.
Every time he shits he shits bricks,
Hence the pyramids and Stanford University.

Chorus:

And in the next cage, we have the elephant
Who, strange enough, holds intercourse
But once each hundred years; but when—he—do—
HE DO!—and how he does enjoy it!

Chorus:

And in the next cage, we have the rhinoceros
The wealthiest animal alive. His name comes from
Rhino meaning money, and *sore ass* meaning piles—
Hence, piles of money. See his ass in the bank.

Chorus:

INVITATION

Anonymous

(From Anecdota Americana—Humphrey Adams, Boston.)

There are so many feather beds,
So many little maiden heads,
There's practically no excuse
For sodomy or self-abuse.

———

GRECIAN BARDS

Anonymous

When Grecian bards caressed their lyres
  We know what else the Greeks caressed,
For there were no suppressed desires
  When Grecian bards caressed their lyres,
And sudden swift erotic fires
  Could kindle in the human breast
When Grecian bards caressed their lyres.
  We know what else the Greeks caressed!

———

MARY'S MAIDENHEAD

A. E. GOLIGHTLY

Mary had a maiden-head;
  She cherished it most dearly;
But since she took a boy to bed,
  It's acted up most queerly.

155

LIMERICKS

I.

There once was a maid in Duluth,
A striver, and seeker of truth;
   This pretty wench
   Was adept at French,
And said all else was uncouth.

II.

There was an old man from Bengal,
Who swore he had only one ball;
   But two sons-of-bitches
   Took down his britches,
And found he had no balls at all.

III.

JACK LONDON

There was a young man of Natal
Who was fucking a hottentot gal;
   She said, "You're a sluggard."
   He said, "You be buggered,
I want to fuck slow, and I shall."

IV.

There was a young man named Hughes,
Who swore off all kinds of booze;
   He said, "When I'm muddled
   My senses get fuddled,
And I pass up too many screws."

156

V.

Love letters no longer they write us,
To their homes they so seldom invite us;
   It grieves me to say,
   They have learned with dismay,
We can't cure their *vulva pruritis*.

VI.

There was an old lady from France,
Who hopped a train in a trance;
   The engineer fucked her,
   So did the conductor,
And the brakeman went off in his pants.

VII.

There was a young Frenchman from Brest,
Who sucked off young girls with zest;
   In spite of their howls,
   He sucked on their bowels,
And spit all the shit on their breast.

VIII.

There was a young man from Marseilles,
Who lived on clap juice and snails;
   When tired of these
   He lived upon cheese
From his prick, which he picked with his nails.

IX.

There was a young girl from Lancaster,
Who'd do anything anybody asked her;
   But when she got spliced
   She got so high-priced
Only Jesus H. Christ and John Jacob Astor.

X.

There was an old man from Robles,
Who went out to dine with some nobles;
   He would risk his life,
   And fucked the host's wife
And now, so 'tis said, he has no balls.

XI.

There was a young man of Cape Cod,
Who once put my wife into pod;
   His name it was Tucker,
   The dirty old fucker,
The bugger, the blighter, the sod.

XII.

There was a young girl named LeHay,
Who was put in the family way,
   By the mate of a lugger,
   An ignorant bugger,
Who always spelt cunt with a K.

XIII.

There was a young fellow named Charteris,
Put his hand where his young lady's garteris;
   Said she, "I don't mind;
   Up higher you'll find
The place where my pisser and farteris."

XIV.

There was a young lady of Barking Creek,
Who used to have monthlies twice a week;
   A fellow from Woking
   Said, "How provoking,
You don't get any poking so to speak."

XV.

There was a young fellow named Buckingham,
Wrote a pamphlet on women and fuckingham;
   But a clever young turk,
   Eclipsed this great work,
With a volume on assholes and suckingham.

XVI.

There was a young fellow—a banker,
Had bubo, itch, pox, and chancre;
   He got all the four
   From a dirty old whore,
So he wrote her a letter to thank her.

XVII.

There was a young man of Datchet,
Who cut off his prick with a hatchet;
   Then very politely
   He sent it to Whitely,
And ordered a cunt that would match it.

XVIII.

There was a young man of Vinsizes,
Whose bollocks were different sizes;
   His prick, when at ease,
   Hung down to his knees,
Now, what must it be when it rises?

XIX.

There was a monk from Siberia,
Whose life grew weary and wearia;
   At last he did yell,
   As he jumped from his cell,
And buggered the Mother Superia.

XX.

There was an old lady from Grott,
Who lived on green apples and snot;
　　When she couldn't get these,
　　She lived on the cheese
She scraped from the end of her twat.

XXI.

There was an old man from Nantucket,
Whose cock was so long he could suck it;
　　He said with a grin,
　　As he wiped off his chin,
"If my ear was a cunt I could fuck it."

XXII.

I love her in the evening gown,
I love her in her nightie;
　　But when moonlight flits
　　Between her tits,
Jesus Christ, almighty!

XXIII.

There was a young man of Bombay,
Who moulded a cunt out of clay,
　　But the heat of his prick
　　Turned the clay into brick,
And wore all his foreskin away.

XXIV.

There was a young lady from Clyde,
Who'd no ticket on which to ride,
　　So she told the conductor
　　Who immediately fucked her,
And gave her two dollars beside.

XXV.

There was a young man from Kent
Whose prick was so long it bent,
  To save himself trouble
  He put it in double,
And instead of coming he went.

XXVI.

There was a young lady from Lichen
Was scratching her cunt in the kitchen;
  Her mother said, "Rose,
  It's crabs I suppose"—
"Yes, and by Jesus, they're itchin'."

XXVII.

There was a young girl from Anhuyser
Who said that no man could surprise her,
  But Pabst took a chance,
  Found Schlitz in her pants,
And now she is sadder Budweiser.

XXVIII.

There was a young man from Montrose
Who screwed himself with his toes:
  He could do it so neat
  He fell in love with his feet,
And christened them Myrtle and Rose.

XXIX.

There was a man from Montclair
Who was screwing his girl on a chair;
  At the twenty-first stroke
  The little chair broke,
And his gun went off in the air.

XXX.

There was a man from Belgravia
Who thought he was the Saviour;
    He went down the Strand
    With his cock in his hand,
And was nabbed for indecent behavior.

XXXI.

There was a young man from Brighton
Who thot he'd at last found a tight-un;
    He said, "Oh my love,
    It fits like a glove"—
She said, "You're not in the right-un."

XXXII.

There was an Emir of Algiers
Who said to his harem, "My dears,
    You may think it odd of me
    But I've given up sodomy,
Tonight there'll be fucking."—Loud cheers.

XXXIII.

There was a young girl from Detroit
Who at fucking was very adroit;
    She could contract her vagina
    To a pin-point or fina',
Or widen it out like a quoit.

XXXIV.

There was an old bird of Dundee
Who went on a hell of a spree;
    He wound up the clock
    With the end of his cock,
And diddled his wife with the key.

XXXV.

There was a young man named Dave
Who screwed a dead whore in a cave;
  When asked if ashamed
  He said, "I can't be blamed,
Just think of the money I've saved."

XXXVI.

There was a young woman of Lynn
Whose mother would keep her from sin;
  So she filled up her crack
  With cement and shellac,
But the men took it out with a pin.

XXXVII.

There was a young lady named Wild
Who for years remained undefiled
  Through thinking of Jesus
  And venereal diseases,
And the danger of being with child.

XXXVIII.

There was an old man named Grasty
Whose favorite sport was ass-ty;
  He'd bugger with joy
  Any innocent boy,
But thought fornication was nasty.

XXXIX.

There was a young lady named Hester
Who said to the man who undressed her:
  "If you don't mind
  Please enter behind,
The front is beginning to fester."

XL.

There was a young man from Yale
Who was exceedingly pale,
   He spent his vacation
   In self masturbation,
Because of the high price of tail.

XLI.

There was a young plumber named Leigh
Was plumbing his girl by the sea;
   Said Leigh, still plumbing,
   "I hear someone coming."
Said she, "Don't worry, it's me."

XLII.

There was a young lady named White
Found herself in a terrible plight;
   A fellow named Tucker
   Struck her, the fucker,
The bugger, the bastard, the shite!

XLIII.

There was an old fellow of Greenwich
Who lived upon cabbage and spinach;
   He had such a tool
   It wound on a spool,
In-ich by in-ich by in-ich!

XLIV.

There was an old maid from Racine
Who invented a fucking machine,
   Concave or convex,
   To suit either sex,
And remarkably easy to clean.

XLV.

There was an old man of Peru
Who found he had nothing to do,
So he went to the garret
And lay with the parrot,
And sent the result to the zoo!

XLVI.

There once was a man of St. Clair
Who tried to bugger a bear,
But the nasty old brute
Took a snatch as his root,
And left nothing but bollocks and hair.

XLVII.

A young Juliet of St. Louis
On a balcony stood, acting screwy;
Her Romeo climbed
But he wasn't well timed,
And when half way up, off he went—blooey!

XLVIII.

There once was a maid of Costanza
And her box it was big as Bonanza,
It was nine inches deep
And the sides were quite steep—
It had whiskers like General Carranza.

XLIX.

There was a young lady at sea
Who said, "God, how it hurts me to pee."
"I see," said the mate,
"That accounts for the state
Of the captain, the purser, and me."

L.

There was an old maid of Twickenham
Who took all the cocks without picken' 'em:
    She knelt on the sod
    And prayed to her God,
To lengthen, and strengthen, and thicken 'em!

LI.

There once was a kiddie named Carr
Caught a man on top of his mar;
    As he saw him stick 'er,
    He said with a snicker,
"You do it much faster than par."

LII.

There was a young lady named May
Who frigged herself in the hay;
    She bought a pickle—
    One for a nickel—
And wore all the warts away!

LIII.

There was a young man named Paul
Whose cock was exceedingly small;
    He buggered a bug
    On the edge of a rug,
And the bug didn't know it at all.

LIV.

There was a young lady named Eva
Filled up the bath tub to receiv-a;
    She took off her clothes
    From her head to her toes,
And a voice at the keyhole yelled, "Beaver!"

LV.

A wonderful fish is the flea,
He bores and he bites on me;
   I would love, indeed,
   To watch him feed,
But he bites me where I cannot see.

LVI.

In Spring Miss May marries Perse,
'Til then their pash' they disburse:
   With a thin piece of rubber
   There's no need to scrub 'er—
Of course, there's no harm to rehearse.

LVII.

There was a young lady named Min
Who thought that to love was a sin;
   But when she was tight
   It seemed quite all right,
So everyone filled her with gin.

LVIII.

There was an old man of Decatur
Took out his red-hot pertater;
   He tried at her dent
   But when his thing bent,
He got down on his knees and he ate 'er.

LIX.

There was a young girl in Ohia
Whose baptismal name was Maria;
   She would put on airs
   And pee on the stairs,
If she thot that no one was nigh 'er.

LX.

There was an old lady named Tucket
Who went to hell in a bucket;
   When she did get there
   And they asked her for fare,
She lifted her skirts and said, "Suck it!"

LXI.

There was an old maid of Wheeling
Who had a most terrible feeling;
   She lay on her back
   And opened her crack,
And pissed right up at the ceiling.

LXII.

There was a fat lady of Bryde
Whose shoestrings once came untied;
   She didn't dare stoop
   For fear she would poop,
And so she cried, and cried, and cried.

LXIII.

A skinny old maid named Dunn
Wed a short-peckered sun-of-a-gun;
   She said, "I don't care,
   If there isn't much there,
God knows it is better than none."

LXIV.

A princess who ruled in Algiers
Had bushels of dirt in her ears:
   The tail of her shirty
   Was also quite dirty,
She never had washed it in years.

LXV.

There was an old woman named Croft
Who amused herself in a loft;
   She said, "A bologna
   Is the real corona,
Because it never gets soft."

LXVI.

There was a young man of Tagore
Who had just an inch, no more;
   'Twas alright for keyholes
   And little girls' peeholes,
But it wasn't so good for a whore.

LXVII.

There was a young lady named Myrtle
She went to bed with a turtle;
   She had crabs, so they say,
   In a year and a day,
Which proves that the turtle was fertile.

LXVIII.

There was a man from Equador
Went to bed with a bally whore;
   He got up in the dark
   And was heard to remark.
"I hired a twat, not a corridor."

LXIX

There was a young lady in Natches
Who fell in some nettle-wood patches;
   She sits in her room
   With her bare little moon,
And scratches, and scratches, and scratches.

LXX.

There was a young lady named Maud
A terrible society fraud;
   In company, I'm told,
   She was awfully cold,
But if you got her alone, Oh God!

LXXI.

There was a young man from Lynn
Whose cock was the size of a pin;
   Said his girl with a laugh
   As she felt of his staff,
"This won't be much of a sin."

LXXII.

There was a young dame in Devises
Whose twat was several sizes;
   Once it was small—
   Of no use at all—
But now it takes several prizes.

LXXIII.

There was a young lady of Wheeling
Said to her beau, "I've a feeling
   My little brown jug
   Has need of a plug"—
And straightway she started to peeling.

LXXIV

There was an old man from Roop
Had lost control of his poop:
   While dining on day
   His good wife did say,
"Stop making that noise with your soop."

LXXV.

There was a young maid of Klepper
Went out one night with a stepper;
   And now in dismay
   She murmurs each day,
"His pee-pee was made of red-pepper!"

LXXVI.

There once was a girl from Celesia
Who said, "If my twat don't please ya,
   And if you don't mind,
   You may try my behind—
But be careful my tapeworm don't seize ya."

LXXVII.

There was a young lady in Brent:
When her old man's pecker it bent,
   She said with a sigh,
   "Oh, why must it die?
Let's fill it with Portland Cement."

LXXVIII.

A young Swede who felt like a Turk
Fell asleep one night after work:
   He had a wet dream,
   But awoke, it would seem,
In time to give it a yerk.

LXXIX.

There was a young lady of Ipswith
Took grain to the mill to get grist with;
   But the miller's son Jack
   Put her on her back,
And united the things that they pissed with.

LXXX.

There was an old man in Goditch
Had the gon, the syph and the itch;
 His name was McNabs—
 He also had crabs,
The dirty old son-of-a-bitch.

LXXXI.

There was an old maid from Gloucester
Met a passionate man who tossed her;
 She wasn't much hurt,
 But it dirtied her skirt,
So think of the anguish it cost 'er.

LXXXII.

There was an old maid in Exeter
Dearly loved to nibble a peter;
 She often would say,
 "I like it this way
For I think it's very much neater."

LXXXIII.

An innocent boy in Lapland
Was told that frigging was grand;
 But at his first trial
 He said with a smile,
"I've had the same feeling by hand."

LXXXIV.

A girl who lived in Kentucky
Said, "Yes, I've been awfully lucky,
 No man ever yet
 On my back made me get,
But sometimes I feel awful fucky."

LXXXV.

A coon who was out with his Liz
Said, "Baby, let's get down to biz."
   Said she, "That cain't be,
   Less you'se stronger'n me,
But, honey, I reckon you is."

LXXXVI.

Winter is here with his Grouch:
The time when you sneeze and slouch;
   You can't take your women
   Canoein' or swimmin',
But a lot can be done on a couch.

LXXXVII.

There was a young lady of Lynn
In a bed with an old man named Wynn;
   Tho he tried his best
   And diddled with zest,
She kept asking, "My love, is it in?"

LXXXVIII.

When she wanted a new way to futter
He greased her behind with butter;
   Then, with a sock,
   In went his jock,
And they carried her home on a shutter.

LXXXIX

Full ninety years old was Lynn
When he went to a hookshop to sin;
   But try as he would
   It did him no good,
For all he had left was the skin.

XC.

There was a young woman in Dee
Who stayed with each man she did see;
    When it came to a test
    She wished to be best,
And practice makes perfect, you see.

XCI.

There was a young lady in Maine
Who had a young man on the brain;
    He swore he was true
    But, between me and you,
He fooled her again and again.

XCII.

There was a young man of Ostend
Who let a girl play with his end;
    She took hold of Rover
    And looked it over,
And it did what she didn't intend.

XCIII.

There was a young lady of Hub
Went with her beau to a pub,
    But her mamma spied her,
    To the bathroom hied her,
And Oh, how she made that girl scrub!

XCIV.

I am the King of Siam,
For women I don't give a damn;
    You may think it odd of me
    But I prefer sodomy,
What a hell of a bugger I am!

XCV.

There was a young girl from Gloucester
Whose people thought they had lost her;
   But they found in the grass
   The marks of her ass,
And the knees of one who had crossed 'er.

XCVI.

There was a young dolly named Molly
Who thought that to frig was folly;
   Said she, "Your pee-pee
   Means nothing to me
But, I'll do it just to be jolly."

XCVII.

Becky who was engaged to a tailor
Went out one night with a sailor;
   "Oh, my gawsh!" said her ma.
   "Oi, Oi!" said her pa,
"It's too late but I'll soitenly whale 'er."

XCVIII.

There was a cute girl from Madrid
Who was naughty in all that she did;
   She played strip-pkoer
   Until it broke her,
Which made her a popular kid.

XCIX

TO HELEN

Said she, "I'm sick of my mate,
And marriage, I think's out of date;
   I long to be captive,
   For I know I'm adaptive,
So violets I choose for my Fate."

C.

"Competition is keen, you'll agree,"
Said an ancient old flapper from Dee,
    So she dyed her gray tresses,
    Chopped a foot from her dresses,
And her *reason* you plainly can see.

CI.

There was a young fellow from Eno
Who said to his girl, "Now, old Beano,
    Lift your skirt up in front,
    And enlarge your old cunt,
For the size of this organ is keen-o."

CII.

There was a young man from Cape Horn
Who wished he had never been born;
    Nor would he have been
    If his parents had seen
That the end of the rubber was torn.

CIII.

There was a young fellow named Louvies,
Who tickled his girl in the boovies,
    And as she contorted,
    He looked down and snorted,
"My prick wants to get in your movies!"

AUTHOR AND TITLE INDEX

INDEX—*Continued*

INDEX—*Continued*

INDEX—*Continued*

INDEX—*Continued*

INDEX—*Continued*